Ho\

Sub Title

How to Detect and Defeat Todays Spy Technology

Written By

Daniel Hanson Jr

Copyright© protected 2015/2017 by:

Silver Palace Enterprises

ISBN: 9781548762452

Chapters

Introduction

I am not attempting to feed off of anyone's paranoia but am providing this material to educate the general public about the technology that can be used by predators to victimize you. This is simply for information purposes and I make every effort to insure this does not become a how-to book. This will not change the number of rapists out there. After 9/11, no one should think our world will ever be the same again. Crime is rampant and the public needs to be informed of how criminals can go about their business as well as sexual assault.

This book is about preventing sexual assault and the technology that can be used against everyone for that purpose. I am not playing the blame the victim game. There have always been rapists but I can't somehow wonder if there would be fewer of them were parents allowed to discipline their children correctly today. There is no justification for rape but you the victim need to be educated on how to prevent it from happening to you.

A woman asked me "Can you prevent rape?" Every time a rapist goes to prison another rape has been prevented. You can prevent it from happening to you also. Of 50 serial killers 26% reported being sexually abused as children. Many rapists were also sexually abused as children. I once created a petition at Whitehouse.gov to make chemical castration mandatory for predators of children 14 and younger. Breaking this cycle of violence is a very good way of preventing rape.

Shame on any society that does not take measures to protect its children.

It is not my intention to inform anyone about how to spy on others but to inform the general public about what can be done to them and how to defeat it. The devices discussed here can/are being used to sexually assault women. Some material has been included to make you more aware of just how dangerous your world really is. I need to remove any naivety you have that rape can't happen to you. Seek out a missing persons list and you will see that the majority are female. Wal-Mart has one for a start.

Being old enough to remember the Iranian hostage crisis, I recall laughing at the paranoia of the Iranians when a television reporter filmed a double-walled glass house that they had constructed to keep the U.S. from spying on them. Looking back now, I marvel at my naiveté and believe that in this day of identity theft and crime it is time to open the eyes of the general public to what methods exist to spy on them.

This material will focus on exposing the technology that can be used to spy on us and will discuss the anti-spy technology that is available. Invasion of privacy is a crime for which few people are prosecuted. The difficulty is in the fact that this crime leaves very few tell-tale trails to follow. Consequently, to be able to prove the crime, the criminal must be caught in the act. This material will improve your chances of that.

When I was sixteen, a seventeen-year-old was caught tapping into someone's phone line. Fortunately, for this character, the people were not willing to prosecute him, but this proves how easy it is to obtain the information and equipment to do this. If a seventeen-year-old can do it anyone else certainly can!

One last thing before we delve into the world of spying. I want to make you very aware that this happens. There are many companies in the U.S. and abroad making money selling this technology. A good portion of P.I. time is spent investigating cheating spouses.

They do not achieve the results they do with-out bending the rules a lot. I have a friend who wanted me to go with him to tail people on worker's comp. He was very gung-ho until I pointed out that these were people just like himself, who had been on worker's comp not too long ago. I know someone who was on unemployment that was investigated as well. You will never know when you are being spied upon, and this is not to create any paranoia. Just how many people who have been the victim of a violent crime were stalked by their attacker using today's technology? It is essential to learn how to detect and defeat this technology.

This material is for informational purposes only and its size is not what you are paying for.

It is a very good thing I am on the right side of the law. If not, I could be a very dangerous person. I am not making any confession in anything I print. These are real cases of which I have personal experience, or that I remember from the media.

As I mention I have attempted to get some laws passed by starting petitions at WWW.Whitehouse.gov. They all failed. Sadly, they do not make it easy, deliberately. You need 150 signatures before your petition will even show up in the list available to the general public on their site. I still find it hard to believe that I could not collect 100 thousand signatures from woman to put chemical castration on the law books.

Feel free to create your own petitions if you have any ideas of some laws that would help reduce violent sexual crimes. At least I did more than just write a book about it. Maybe the feminists could actually do something useful for a change. They certainly have the number of followers to get something done. Liberating people form sexual crimes would certainly do a lot for our world. Want to know more about what the feminist are truly liberating women from read my other book titled "God's Feminist Movement". Definitely not written by a woman.

Bionic Ears

During the Seventies, with the desire for alternate sources of energy, a few advocated cooking food by using mirrors to increase the concentration of the sun's rays. Today there seems to be a resurgence of this, especially in India. This took a very long time to work, and in the process of waiting a brave or stupid few realized that they could cook themselves. Not really, but they did try to get a tan this way. So today perhaps we have a lot of tanning booths thanks to this desire. Don't rush out and try to tan yourselves this way. Skin cancer is up by 36 per cent today and this is a sure way to increase your chances of getting it. It will also increase your chances of getting those brown spots.

Remember the large Satellite dishes during the 80's and the smaller ones popping up on houses later. The shape of the dish mathematically is known as a parabola. What this shape does is reflect all radio waves hitting anywhere on its entire surface to a focal point, where the amplifier is placed.

Therefore, we have learned that we can increase the strength of the sun's rays and radio waves. Then someone along the way realized that a parabola could be used to increase the strength of sound waves too. A formula exists to find the size of the parabola that gives a decibel (dB) gain of 27. Of course, you can also amplify the microphone signal. This is great for stage work but is illegal for listening to your neighbors.

I had a college math professor who told us how he used to listen to his neighbors at their parties talking about him. Fortunately, he stopped when I told him how illegal this was and how much prison time he could get.

These are nothing but a microphone with a special curved device that increases the range with which the microphone can pick up voices.

The bad news is that that range can be extended to half a mile (or to miles in some cases). The limitations on this are that you need a good line of sight and low wind without a lot of interference noise. The bad news is that someone could listen to you without you knowing it. Buy a good set of binoculars for the day, and a night scope for the night. That could still prove iffy.

Take a picture for evidence should you catch someone pointing one at you. The only legal use for these is if you are a bird-watcher or want to track animals in the woods. They are illegal for deer hunting and fall into the illegal electronic locating device category. They may also be of some help in search and rescue.

I have not heard of any counter measures for these devices. Even whispering will not help. There are white noise generators that are built to make electronic bugs difficult to hear with but I do not know what effect they will have here. Do an internet search for Audio Jammers – these generate a random masking sound that disables any nearby microphone. The ones I have found are not cheap. If you want to make your own and are electrically inclined do a search for a schematic of white or pink noise generators. More expensive acoustic generators come with transducers that are attached to walls and ceilings will jam mics without introducing noise in the environment you are in. Meaning you will not have to shout over the noise which defeats the purpose of making the noise in the first place. You also can find Cd's that have white noise on them to play.

Showers also muffle sound picked up by electronic bugs, or you could use the Cone of Silence that Maxwell Smart would use, definitely extreme. Like I said else ware most stuff available to the public is lame. The best I have seen for these is a range of 300 yards. Not near enough to be out of sight. Yes, the pros have access to far better.

Bugs

Electronic bugs that is. Some can be remotely turned on and off to aid battery life and possibly to avoid detection. In the 1980s, we (USA) were building an embassy in Russia. We had to tear it down because they were putting these in the cement. It is impossible to change the batteries once the cements sets. These get their power from radio waves, a radio station transmitting tower and your radio antenna act just like a transformer. Radio waves for a transmitting tower induce a signal into the receiving antenna. Radio waves like light are a form of energy. Advances in electronic circuit design have reduced the size of electronic components. Meaning electronic bugs have gotten smaller and smarter. Now some can be hidden inside padded mail envelopes. They even come disguised as pens nowadays. It has been done before this but an article in Engineering on the Edge (November 2014) discussed how Stanford University Engineers created and ant sized radio that gathers its power from the electromagnetic waves that carry signals to its receiving antenna.

Panasonic is making a new small rechargeable battery suitable for pen shaped devices. Can you say, "video spy pen." It will also provide high output required for near field communications. It is slim and its length about the width of a penny which it was pictured with. I cannot help but wonder what else it could be used in. Think of a device that sits in a base that is charged from the base but does not plug into it. Say an ultrasonic tooth brush.

All electrical wires emit a field when energized. This is called Electromagnetic Induction, it is the principle that is used to charge you tooth brush. There is a coil of wire inside the base and another inside the toothbrush. First thing I thought of is, could this battery be charged by placing it next to a power cord say inside a lamp?

Years ago, it was big with some companies that they could control equipment etc. using their electrical wiring. Special filters blocked the AC with an injected radio-frequency signal that traveled down the line and issued the desired action. Hotels used to like them to turn on the heat etc. in a room from the main office. These can also be used to eavesdrop on a target. The signal could be picked up with a receiver. These can be installed in any electrical socket and are very difficult to detect. The best method is to get down on your hands and knees and remove the covers from all sockets and switches to ensure there is nothing else in them.

Both bugs and phone taps that transmit a signal do so in several ranges: UHF, FM, AM, VHF and microwave frequencies. Some are even able to scramble the transmission. Some transmit an infrared signal. One manufacturer advertises theirs as so small to make the olive mike look like an elephant. It has a range of 0.6 miles. They come in all shapes and forms

Some electronic bugs are voice activated to conserve the batteries. And the receiver can be attached to a voice activated tape recorder concealed in the trunk of a car parked in the neighborhood eliminating the stake out.

A bug concealed in a lamp can have an uninterrupted power supply as long as the lamp is plugged in, being on is not a requirement. Although being plugged in is important if the predator wants to hear what goes on when the light goes out.

Cheap ways to detect an electronic bug

Take a radio apart, carefully. Adjust the trimmer cap on the back of the channel adjustment knob. It will take trial and error to find the trimmer cap you need to adjust. You will have to try them all as they are not marked. For example, FM radio signals operate in the 88 to 108 Megahertz range. At 109 Megahertz, the airliners take over.

Most FM bugs will use this area between 108 – 109 for transmission or at the lower end of FM from 78 to 88 Megahertz. No one's radio is tuned to receive them, making them undetectable by the general public. Remember, I said the pros have the top of the line stuff. FM is for the amateurs. So just take this with a grain of salt for information purposes. These are the more readily available flavors though.

Tune your radio to a station at the top end of the dial. Adjust the trimmer cap so that the location of the channel will walk up the scale on the dial.

It will take some practice to determine which way to turn the cap. Make an adjustment, then readjust the radio dial to find the channel again. You are turning the right way if the channel is now closer to the end of the channel indicator. Continue until you are confident that you will now be able to hear in the desired range of 108 to 109 Megahertz. Note that you will have to tune the dial slowly so you do not skip over a bug. The cheaper the radio, the worse the results will be. Also note that this will only tell you if there are any bugs in that frequency of FM that you have available, which will not cover all the types of bugs available. Nor will this aid you in locating a bug if you should discover one. This will make for a fun experiment anyways, and should you find one, I suggest buying a true detector that will enable you to find it. Look for one that will work in the Gigahertz range. If you are handy with soldering and electronics, there are various kits available.

A cheap method of making a bug give off it presence is to make it squeal. You know like a radio will sometimes do when someone calls in to a radio station and forgets to turn down their radio. That is called feedback. Anyway, one of those pain field generators emits a high ultrasonic frequency that may make them squeal, giving themselves away.

I recommend buying a proper bug detector if you really want to find any bugs. Of course, private detectives can also perform this service for you for a fee. On the other hand, if they are the ones bugging you, don't expect them to find their own. Remember, they do not achieve the results they do by not bending the rules once in a while.

One problem with hiring a PI to do a sweep is that the first time you leave your home/office empty it can be bugged again.

Here is a bug detector I recommend. Available at www.counter-surveillance.com, model MCD-22H Works up to 9 Gigahertz. Then you can check your house car or where ever you want anytime. Wish they were paying me for telling you this. They do not have an affiliate program so if you buy it anywhere else you are just paying for the middleman's markup.

Chemical/Biological Weapons

Probably and hopefully, the average person will not encounter any of these, since this material is about what people can do, we will examine them briefly. No one should have forgotten the anthrax in the mail incident. Fortunately, this is not easily created and well out of the reach of the average Joe. However, Ricin has been making headlines over the past few years. Ricin has been involved in several incidents, including the high-profile assassination of Georgi Markov using an umbrella (Wikipedia).

And then there is the guy who was staying in the extended stay hotel with some Ricin that he had made. He had some scheme for poisoning his enemies but ended up poisoning himself. He was lucky I guess; he lived but got arrested in the end. Even one of the police officers was exposed when he entered the room. Most disturbing was to watch on television only a few days later an official of the U.S. government describe how easy it is to make. Not something anyone needs to hear. Do not even be curious about this. It is one of the deadliest poisons man can create. It has no cure and sufficient amounts will always lead to death. Recently a college student was found with some in his dorm room. It's out there. I have gotten more than one catalog in the mail that had the main ingredient for Ricin available.

Let us not forget the people putting arsenic into pill bottles in the 1980s, which is why we have tamper-resistant pill and food containers today. In April 2013, a California woman planted two bottles of tainted orange juice at a San Jose Starbucks. She was charged with attempted murder,

Sarin is a nerve agent discovered by German Scientists in 1938 while trying to make a better pesticide. A single drop of Sarin the size of a pinhead can kill an adult. The cult leader who ordered the 1995 Sarin attacks in Japan's subways where thirteen people died received the death penalty.

Doors/Windows

According to the "Burglary of Single Family Houses" guide, published by the U.S. Department of Justice's Office of Community Oriented Policing Services (COPS) in one third of burglaries they came in through an open window or door. If you happen to be home it can/will turn into a rape. As I have said else ware beware of arrogant people. Burgling some one's home takes arrogance.

A person's ability to be safe and secure in their own homes should be first and foremost on your to do list. Rapes; murders and kidnappings all happen in the home. I strongly recommend getting a gun. You are your first line of defense. Get an alarm system. They are far less costly than being raped in your own home. They also provide peace of mind when you are away. I seriously advocate installing interior/exterior cameras with recording ability that will interact with the alarm. Then it will not be just your word against theirs.

Most burglars will go to your back door, lots less obvious to the neighbors. Put motion sensing lights there. Also, trim tree branches up to six feet from the ground and shrubs down to below window sills eliminating something to hide behind. If you get a choice in your doors, do not choose one with a large window. They are easily smashed out. If you are constructing a house, see if you can get the contractor to use hardwood around the door casing.

Often a burglar will force the casing but not the door itself. Working with a friend, we installed a door once in a cellar and put a small piece of wood between the lock and cement wall to eliminate movement of the casing. Later, the owners told my friend that this had prevented a burglar from breaking in.

Use electronic timers for lights when you are away. It will confuse burglars and hopefully make them move on. Also stop your mail and newspaper subscriptions.

Now to discuss locks, no lock is pick proof. Some are just harder than others. No requirement that you must be a locksmith to acquire picks. I also found a website dedicated to picking locks free to everyone. No, I am not going to give you the URL. It has been said that locks just keep honest people honest. There is not a lock made that cannot be picked. Be aware that in some states it is illegal to even own a lock pick unless you are a locksmith.

I was waiting for a woman in a restaurant on a date when she came in and showed me something she had picked up in the parking lot. It was a tension spring from a lock-picking kit. I wiped her prints off it and threw it in the trash. Whereupon the receptionist picked it out and called the police. They let her go when I explained she did not know what it was.

I knew some people who had their home burgled while they slept (and they slept with their doors locked). There were 5 such burglaries in my neighborhood all in one night. I am still waiting to see what happens if someone wakes up during the burglary. The solution to that is to get some sort of alarm even it is only for the door or window, especially if you are traveling.

Some years ago, there was a man in my city who went around trying doors at night. If he found one unlocked, he went in and raped the woman who was at home. Always lock your doors to your home and car; not every rapist will have lock picks. So, you live alone you are sound asleep and suddenly you feel a hand over your mouth. You never heard a thing because you did not get a door alarm. What do you do if you do have an alarm and it wakes you? A. Dial 911 if you have time and hope they arrive in time. B. Reach for a gun. C. All of the above.

A special lock that will fit through a hotel door that you can lock on the inside is available. Google "Hotel Door Lock" for a supplier. I have never seen one available at a hardware store. Buy one if you travel. Also, get yourself one of those small door alarms. Double sided tape will help attach them when travelling. These are readily available at department and hardware stores and are relatively cheap. There is also a "Super Door Stop Alarm" that you jam under the door.

Use high quality locks and dead bolts on solid exterior doors. Dead bolts are rated grade 1 2 or 3. You get what you pay for. Grade 1 Provides the best residential security available Knobs – must withstand 80K cycles 6 door strides and 360-pound weight test. Dead bolts must withstand 10 door strikes. Grade 2 Meets light commercial and exceeds residential building requirements it passes 250 weight tests and 5 hammer strikes. Grade 3 Meets residential building requirements only provides minimal residential security with just 150 pound tests and 2 strikes. Do a search on the internet for "Charley Bar" it is a portable bar to be put in a sliding glass door; use it when you are traveling. I have never liked sliding glass doors; way too much glass.

Also, when staying in a Hotel or Motel unplug the TV when you are not watching it. It is a limitless source of power for an electronic bug and or a camera to leach off. Your phone can be listened in on even when on the hook. Unplug it if you so desire. I know of rapes that have happened at Motels.

Peeping

Companies also make and sell various fiber optics, which can be used to see under or over doors and through keyholes. By the way, if you live in an older house, where many of the locks have old skeleton keys, take the locks apart and cover the inside hole with black tape. Better yet, replace them because only two types were ever made. I remember watching one of those sitcoms where the mother found out her kids and the neighborhood kids were watching her and her husband. Of course, that happens in real life all too often. Locking the doors will also prevent you from being walked in on too.

Have no doubt that what the criminals want they will get. I have known of several instances where criminals have managed to acquire police radios.

I suggest using something to block the inside of those peepholes in the doors. The peephole will enable a burglar to have a quick look at everything he would want to steal with a reverse peeper. I recently found one similar reverse peeper for $23; very easy to get. I cannot think of one reason a law-abiding citizen would need one for.

Or if you are like me and have been divorced and have nothing to steal don't worry about it. As I was leaving one night and turning on my porch light, my neighbor told me I was just advertising to a burglar that I was not home. I told him that after getting divorced I have nothing left to steal. A peeping Tom would also want one. Criminals have been using these before the police.

There are also under the door audio and video viewers. As well as flexible endoscopes designed to work through small apertures like key holes or small holes through walls. Kind of like when watching a movie and the eyes on a painting move. Seriously!

Garage doors

If you have an automatic garage door opener, you know about the switches that you can use to change the code for your door. Well, with any set number of switches, you can only get so many possible combinations. Someone invented a small hand-held computer called an AGO that will step through all those possible combinations until it finds the right one, thus opening anyone's garage door. Manufacturers will eventually defeat countermeasures, but that will eventually be overcome as well. It's kind of like what Spock said: "Military secrets are the most fleeting of all."

When going away for any amount of time during which you will not be home overnight, shut off your opener. And have a means of mechanically locking your garage door from the inside. While on the subject of garage doors, a good many of them are not too solid to resist penetration. When purchasing one, have this in mind and opt for steel. All too often, homeowners think their garage door is secure and use a weak door to enter their house from the garage. If you don't care that much about your garage, at least secure your home with a strong inner door.

Windows

A means for burglars or anyone else who wants entry to a home. I was in a new home under construction today. I am still amazed at the number of new homes that take no measures to deny access through cellar windows. They are cheap and are not meant to stop illegal entry to your home. A small child could be dropped in through one of them quite easily. Ever see the Charles Dickens movie *Oliver*? A woman was telling me how her home had been burgled and the only way they could have gotten in was through a small window. She could not understand how until I told her that they had to have put a kid through it. Why even bother put a lock on your door if you have no fear of burglars?

During the construction of a new home, holes could be drilled into the cellar window frame and steel rods could be pushed through them so that when the cement sets they will become permanent fixtures. Just make sure there is plenty of the rod sticking past the window frame to anchor in the cement.

I instructed a friend once how to add bars to his cellar windows. Later he told me that someone had tried to break in through one. For an existing home, you will need a masonry drill bit and anchors for the rods. Any hardware store that provides the rods will have brackets in which to hold the rods. If you cannot find a bracket with an end cap to prevent the rods being pushed aside, drill a hole just at the end of each rod and insert a bolt in an anchor to prevent any sideways movement.

Get or make a block that can be set in the track, preventing opening of the window. Get one also for sliding glass doors. In fact, if you are really into feeling secure in your home, opt out of the sliding doors altogether. Glass breaks all too easily.

If you insist on putting bars on your windows, make sure they open from the inside and periodically inspect them. People have been killed in house fires because they could not get out through a barred window during a fire.

From Wikipedia

A **safe room** or **panic room** is a fortified room that is installed in a private residence or business to provide a safe shelter, or hiding place, for the inhabitants in the event of a break-in, home invasion, tornado, terror attack or other threat. Safe rooms usually contain communications equipment, so that law enforcement authorities can be contacted.

Construction techniques

The simplest safe room is simply a closet (Think walk in closet) with the hollow-core door replaced with an exterior-grade solid-core door that has a deadbolt and longer hinge screws and strike-plate screws to resist battering. Sometimes, the ceiling is reinforced, or gated, to prevent easy access from the attic or from an overhead crawl space.

More expensive safe rooms, such as those constructed for celebrities and executives, have walls and a door reinforced with sheets of steel, Kevlar, or bullet-resistant fiberglass. The hinges and strike plate are often reinforced with long screws. Some safe rooms may also have externally vented ventilation systems and a separate telephone connection. They might also connect to an escape shaft.

Safe rooms in the basement can be built with concrete walls, a building technique that is normally not possible on the upper floors of wood-framed structures unless there is substantial structural reinforcement to the building.

The U.S. State Department often uses steel grillwork much like a jail to seal off parts of a home used by U.S. Foreign Service members overseas when they are living in cities with a high crime threat. In some cities, the entire upstairs area is grilled off as well as every window and door to the home.

Other homes have steel doors to one or more bedrooms that can be bolted closed to provide time for security forces to arrive. For strong storms or tornadoes, a storm safe room must be built to withstand high winds and flying debris, even if the rest of the residence becomes severely damaged or destroyed; specific concerns:

- The safe room should be adequately anchored to the foundation to resist overturning and uplift.
- The walls, ceiling, and door of the shelter should withstand wind pressure and resist penetration by windborne objects or falling debris.
- The connections between all parts of the safe room should be strong enough to resist separation by wind.

- Sections of either interior or exterior residence walls which are used as walls of the safe room, should be separated from the structure of the residence so that damage to the residence will not cause damage to the safe room.
- **Features**

- Safe rooms may contain communications equipment, such as a cellular telephone, land-line telephone or an amateur radio transceiver, so that law enforcement authorities can be contacted. There may also be a monitor for external security cameras and an alarm system. In basic safe rooms, a peephole in the door may be used for a similar purpose. Safe rooms are typically stocked with basic emergency and survival items such as a flashlight, blankets, a first-aid kit, water, packaged food, self-defense tools, a gas mask, and a simple portable toilet. Safe rooms can be hidden behind many household features, such as mirrors, wardrobes, bookcases and even fireplaces.

DRUGS

Why include a chapter on drugs when the subject is preventing sexual assault? Well drugs twist the mind and create violent people. Rape is still a crime of violence. My main goal is to help people live a safer life which includes many things. Worn your daughters that drugs cost serious money and a guy is not going to give them to her without wanting/leading to something in return. I am not sure if it is on the rise or you just hear about it more but human trafficking is making the headlines more often. Getting their victims hooked on drugs is one way a trafficker makes their victim dependent on them.

Never go to parties where you do not know a single person. A college co-ed went to one with some acquaintances' she had just met. I will spare you the details. I still remember reading a magazine article in the 80's about a man in a drug induced rage dragging a woman by the hair of her head behind the building at a party and shooting her in the head.

I had an eighth-grade teacher who gave us some very good advice that I remembered and followed. It was plain and simple; if you ever set a drink down in public, do not pick it up again. Years later, when in the Air Force, I set a drink down in the poolroom and walked away from it. After returning to it, I threw it in the trash. To which the guy standing next to me got mad and demanded to know why I had done that. A week later, an MP caught him putting something into someone else's drink.

When I was a freshman in high school, one of my female classmates was, as they say, the hottest girl in school. Even the teachers used to turn and look when she walked down the corridors. Needless to say, all the boys wanted her, but she didn't allow anyone to touch her. She attended the Methodist church and was in the Brownies. She always made the high honor role. The smarter a female is the more important sex is to her.

22

Then I moved and eventually graduated from a different high school. Several years later, I returned to our hometown and was sitting at the lunch counter at J. J. Newberries. The woman who served me behind the counter was a dirty blonde with no shape to speak of and unattractive facial features. One of the other customers spoke to her by her first name, which was the same as the heartthrob of the school. In a small town, some things just never change.

So, when she left, I took a chance and asked the customer who had spoken to her if that was who I suspected she was. He replied that it was. Then he told me that she thought she used to be the hottest thing in school. I told him, "She was – I went to school with her." I asked him what had happened to her good looks. He told me she had gotten involved with two guys who had influenced her to use drugs. Then he gave me a lecture on their hazards, and I told him I had never used them. At that time, I thought the authorities were stretching the truth when they told us drugs could ruin your looks, obviously not.

A little later, I got to thinking that she was probably not making much more than minimum wage and decided to chance one more question. How could she afford drugs working here? The reply was that she was prostituting herself. Here was a young lady who'd had great looks, virtue, and intelligence, but bad communications and company destroyed her. The boys will steal and the girls will prostitute themselves to support any addictions they acquire.

When it comes to drugs and sex I wish I could get a dollar from every parent who has said, "Not mine." Alcohol is considered a drug too; it is just that it is socially accepted. Tell your daughters that "Too much alcohol will make you dance and drop your pants". It's been helping ugly people get laid for decades. It removes inhabitations and impairs your judgment.

In some states, it is illegal to have sex with an intoxicated woman. Not moral either but we are taking about sexual assault. Buy one of those little bottles of alcohol they call nips and have your daughter smell it so she will recognize the smell should someone spike her drink.

One of my nephews died in 2008. He was 24, only about 2 months older than my son. The autopsy concluded that he overdosed on Methamphetamine and alcohol. One spring a couple of boys found a foot sticking out of a snow bank, which turned out to belong to a woman in her late twenties. I heard through the grapevine that she had overdosed at a heroin party and her friends had dumped her on the curb like a piece of trash, some friends. Play with drugs and that is the kind you will get also.

Some drugs will make you paranoid. When my nephew that overdosed was little, his family lived over a fireman who was dealing and using. This made the fireman paranoid and he had his fellow dealers play with the kids to intimidate the boy's parents, even though they were no threat to him.

In the gym at college one day, I ran into one of my classmates and we got to talking. The topic of sex with strangers came up and his attitude was that you "just wear a glove", as he put it. Glove in this case was slang for condom. The disturbing thing that makes me remember this is that he also told me he used to be a junkie and all the friends that he shot up with now had AIDS except him. He called it a miracle. Well let me tell you, I didn't believe it for a minute and you should not either.

Speaking of drugs and sex with strangers, a long time ago (maybe two decades) two prostitutes were found dead in the middle of the street here in Worcester. They were found within twenty minutes of each other and only a few miles apart. Both of their pictures were on the front page of the local paper the very next day. One of them was identified as being HIV positive. It takes more than one day to get Aids test results back so this woman was known to be HIV positive and she certainly knew too. How would you like to be one of the guys that had used her the day before? Play with prostitutes and you take a double risk of getting AIDS or any of the other 30-something sexually transmitted diseases. Not just from multiple sex partners but most of them are supporting a drug habit.

A television show on prostitutes showed how one tested positive for an STD, then it showed her back on the streets still working.

I just watched a video on the Internet about a drug called Salvia that is legal to sell in many states. Parents beware – one child committed suicide because of this drug.

I have a niece who had a friend with the same name – Mindy. This Mindy was used by some drug dealers to lure a guy who owed them money into a car. They took him to a cemetery and murdered him. He had taken drugs from them to sell but someone stole the drugs from him and he could not pay for them. He was murdered for just four hundred dollars.

Sadly, there is another drug called the date rape drug (Rohypnol). A television documentary on the manufacturer of this drug demonstrated that there is no medicinal purpose for it at all. Despite this, the manufacturer (Hoffman-LaRoche) refused to cease making it. The manufacturer had made 100 million dollars from it that particular year. Despite being illegal to even possess it in the US (mandatory 3-year prison sentence), it is very likely quite prolific in many countries. The only thing that the manufacturer agreed to do was put something in it that would turn a drink blue after 20 minutes.

This blue dye and decreased water solubility seems to have been successful so much so that its use seems to have dropped to nil. But it is not gone. Always, always be very careful about where you get your drinks. There are others available despite this.

You, first and foremost must be vigilant to take care of yourself. No one else will do it so well. Never let anyone get or hold drinks for you. This is not just for the women; men have been known to be rolled for their wallets too; and for other purposes also. Sexual assault is not just a woman's problem.

So why would a man buy you drinks anyways? Then again there is the fact that alcohol will make you dance and drop your pants if enough is poured into you. The Center for Women and Families notes that alcohol is the chief concern "For rape which takes place on campuses, alcohol is being used in 90% of cases."

A company named Drink Safe Technology manufactures test strips and coasters to detect the date rape drugs gamma hydroxy-butyrate (GHB) and ketamine. These drugs are tasteless odorless and colorless so you need these tests to detect them. The instructions must be followed for them to be effective. Do a keyword search on a search engine to find them. I recently read someone was considering making fingernail polish that could detect date rape drugs. If woman are anything like most men who do not wash their hands after using the bath room I would suggest another method.

Only go out with a group of trusted friends that have agreed to look out for each other that will not leave you alone to pair up with others. It is not always the person buying you the drink you must be leery of.

I know of one bartender who was caught with about 68 Rohypnol pills. He was using them for himself but bartenders can be paid to slip one in a drink as well. Rumor has it that drinking a lot of cranberry juice can reverse some of the amnesia this drug creates.

These days, the drugs slipping out of pockets and into highball glasses are primarily GHB (or "liquid Ecstasy"), Zolpidem (also known as Ambien), scopolamine, and a few lesser-known benzodiazepines, like temazepam or midazolam.

Rapists look for vulnerability in their victims. Drugs create vulnerability. I read an article on Yahoo in which a female opiate addict said she never knew when she would wake up to someone pulling her pants down. Sometimes she was so drugged she was not even aware. Being homeless only made her situation worse. Drugs lead to unemployment which leads to homelessness.

Tips for Parents
The Truth About Club Drugs

I gleaned this from the FBI.

What Are Raves?

"Raves" are high energy, all-night dances that feature hard pounding techno-music and flashing laser lights. Raves are found in most metropolitan areas and, increasingly, in rural areas throughout the country. The parties are held in permanent dance clubs, abandoned warehouses, open fields, or empty buildings.

Raves are frequently advertised as "alcohol free" parties with hired security personnel. Internet sites often advertise these events as "safe" and "drug free." However, they are dangerously over crowded parties where your child can be exposed to rampant drug use and a high-crime environment. Numerous overdoses are documented at these events.

Raves are one of the most popular venues where club drugs are distributed. Club drugs include MDMA (more commonly known as "Ecstasy"), GHB and Rohypnol (also known as the "date rape" drugs), Ketamine, Metham phetamine (also known as "Meth"), and LSD.

Because some club drugs are colorless, odorless, and tasteless, individuals who want to intoxicate or sedate others in order to commit sexual assaults can add them without detection to beverages.

Rave promoters capitalize on the effects of club drugs. Bottled water and sports drinks are sold at Raves, often at inflated prices, to manage hyperthermia and dehydration. Also found are pacifiers to prevent involuntary teeth clenching, menthol nasal inhalers, surgical masks, chemical lights, and neon glow sticks to increase sensory perception and enhance the Rave experience.

Cool down rooms are provided, usually at a cost, as a place to cool off due to increased body temperature of the drug user.

Don't risk your child's health and safety. Ask questions about where he or she is going and see it for yourself. Don't risk losing your child like Samantha Clark's, a 16-year-old who died in 1999 from a dose of GHB someone put in her drink at a party. In the New York Times article about Clark's death there was a quote from Jennifer M. Granholm, then Michigan's attorney general: "[GHB is] an extremely high priority, in that this substance has popped up at these rave parties, and kids can't detect it in a drink." The victims were "kids," almost exclusively young women; the dosing was sexually predatory in motive; and it was possibly avoidable if you skipped "these rave parties."

A drug assault robs you of the ability to narrate your own experience and leaves a terrifying sense of helplessness.

Never accept an open drink or food from a stranger where ever you are; get it yourself. If you ever step away from it do not come back to it; get some fresh food or drink.

What Are Club Drugs?

Methylenedioxymethamphetamine (MDMA)
Street names: Ecstasy, E, X, XTC, Adam, Clarity, Lover's Speed. An amphetamine-based, hallucinogenic type drug that is taken orally, usually in a tablet or capsule form.

Effects:

- Lasts 3-6 hours.
- Enables dancers to dance for long periods of time.
- Increases the chances of dehydration, hypertension, heart or kidney failure, and increased body temperature, which can lead to death.
- Long-term effects include confusion, depression, sleep problems, anxiety, paranoia, and loss of memory.

Gamma-hydoxybutyrate (GHB)
Street names: Grievous Bodily Harm, G, Liquid Ecstasy, Georgia Home Boy
A central nervous system depressant that is usually ingested in liquid, powder, tablet, and capsule forms.

Effects:

- May last up to 4 hours, depending on the dose used.

- Slows breathing and heart rates to dangerous levels.
- Also has sedative and euphoric effects that begin up to 10-20 minutes from ingestion.
- Use in connection with alcohol increases its potential for harm.
- Overdose can occur quickly-sometimes death occurs.

Methamphetamine

Street names: Speed, Ice, Chalk, Meth, Crystal, Crank, Fire, Glass.A central nervous system stimulant, often found in pill, capsule, or powder form, which can be snorted, injected, or smoked.

Effects:

- Displays signs of agitation, excited speech, lack of appetite, and increased physical activity.
- Often results in drastic weight loss, violence, psychotic behavior, paranoia, and sometimes damage to the heart or nervous system.

Ketamine

Street names: Special K, K, Vitamin K, Cat Valium. An inject able anesthetic used primarily by veterinarians, found either in liquid form or as a white powder that can be snorted or smoked, sometimes with marijuana.

Effects:

- Causes reactions similar to those of PCP, a hallucinatory drug.
- Results in impaired attention, learning, and memory function. In larger doses, it may cause delirium, amnesia, impaired motor function, high blood pressure, and depression.

Rohypnol
Street names: Roofies, Rophies, Roche, Forget-me Pill Tasteless and odorless sedative, easily soluble in carbonated beverages, with toxic effects that are aggravated by concurrent use of alcohol.

Effects:

- Can cause anterograde amnesia, which contributes to Rohypnol's popularity as a "date rape" drug.
- Can cause decreased blood pressure, drowsiness, visual disturbances, dizziness, and confusion.

Lysergic Acid Diethylamide (LSD)

Street names: Acid, Boomers, Yellow Sunshine's Hallucinogen that causes distortions in sensory perception, usually taken orally either in tablet or capsule form. Often sold on blotter paper that has been saturated with the drug.

Effects:

- Are often unpredictable and may vary depending on dose, environment, and the user.
- Causes dilated pupils, higher body temperature, increased heart rate and blood pressure, sweating, dry mouth, and tremors.
- Can cause numbness, weakness, and nausea.
- Long-term effects may include persistent psychosis and hallucinogenic persisting perception disorder, commonly known as "flashbacks."

Know the Signs

Effects of stimulant club drugs, such as MDMA and Methamphetamine:

- Increased heart rate
- Convulsions
- Extreme rise in body temperature
- Uncontrollable movements
- Insomnia
- Impaired speech
- Dehydration
- High blood pressure
- Grinding teeth

Effects of sedative/hallucinogenic club drugs, such as GHB, Ketamine, LSD, and Rohypnol:

- Slow breathing
- Decreased heart rate (Except LSD)
- Respiratory problems
- Intoxication
- Drowsiness
- Confusion
- Tremors
- Nausea

Effects common to all club drugs can include anxiety, panic, depression, euphoria, loss of memory, hallucinations, and psychotic behavior. Drugs, traces of drugs, and drug paraphernalia are direct evidence of drug abuse. Pacifiers, menthol inhalers, surgical masks, and other such items could also be considered indicators.

Where Do You Go for Help?

If you suspect your child is abusing drugs, monitor behavior carefully. Confirm with a trustworthy adult where your child is going and what he or she is doing. Enforce strict curfews.

If you have evidence of club drug use, approach your child when he or she is sober, and if necessary, call on other family members and friends to support you in the confrontation.

Once the problem is confirmed, seek the help of professionals. If the person is under the influence of drugs and immediate intervention is necessary, consider medical assistance. Doctors, hospital substance programs, school counselors, the county mental health society, members of the clergy, organizations such as Narcotics Anonymous, and rape counseling centers stand ready and waiting to provide information and intervention assistance.

For more information, Contact:

Office of Justice Programs
http://ojp.gov/

Office of Juvenile Justice and Delinquency Prevention
http://www.ojjdp.gov/
1-800-638-8736

Office for Victims of Crime
http://ojp.gov/ovc/
1-800-627-6872

Drug Enforcement Administration
www.dea.gov

Center for Substance Abuse Treatment (CSAT)
1-800-662-HELP

Community Anti-Drug Coalitions of America
www.CADCA.org

**Substance Abuse and Mental Health Services
Administration**
http://www.samhsa.gov/

National Institute on Drug Abuse
http://www.drugabuse.gov/

Office of National Drug Control Policy Clearinghouse
1-800-666-3332
www.whitehousedrugpolicy.gov

Substance Abuse Treatment Facility Locator
www.findtreatment.samhsa.gov

Effects of Sexual Assault on Victims

As one rape victim has said "It is no fun to be raped." Realize that at first you will not fully understand the consequences as to what has happened to you. It is not called the silent rage for nothing. That means that later it will have a much more negative influence in your life. Be certain it is not going to go away easily.

I vividly remember a 30-year-old woman crying as she told me she had been raped when she was 12. I have been accused of making too much of rape. I don't think so; there is only making too little of it. It can lead to thoughts of suicide, attempted suicide and suicide. Also, depression, anxiety, PTSD, nightmares alcohol and substance abuse problems and eating disorders. No, I don't think I make too much of it.

It seems that keeping secrets is unhealthy for the brain. Psychologist James Pennebaker studied when rape and incest victims kept their secret inside. He concluded "The act of not discussing or confiding the event with another may be more damaging than having experienced the event per se." (Pennebaker, Traumatic experience) He concluded that when subjects confess or wrote about their deeply held secrets, their health improved, and number of doctor visits went down accompanied with measurable decreases in stress hormones.

A secret results from a rivalry, one part of the brain wants to reveal something and another part does not. (Incognito by David Eagleman) Main reason for not is an aversion to the long-term consequences. This is why people are far more likely to reveal their secrets to a total stranger; especially over the phone. This conflict can be dissipated with none of the fear that a friend will think ill of you or that you may be ostracized. The act of telling a secret can in itself be a solution, however a solution may not be what the teller was after.

Studies show that a supportive reaction from the first person a survivor tells can greatly impact the healing process.

This was taken verbatim from Wikipedia.com

As might be expected, a person who has been raped will generally experience high levels of distress immediately afterward. These feelings may subside over time for some people; however, individually each syndrome can have long devastating effects on rape victims and some victims will continue to experience some form of psychological distress for months or years. It has also been found that rape survivors are at high risk for developing substance use disorders, major depression, generalized anxiety disorder, obsessive-compulsive disorder, and eating disorders.

Common stages of RTS (Rape Trauma Syndrome)

RTS identifies three stages of psychological trauma a rape survivor goes through: the acute stage, the outer adjustment stage, and the renormalization stage. The harm caused to a victim of rape or sexual abuse can never be repaired.

Acute stage

The acute stage occurs in the days or weeks after a rape. Durations vary as to the amount of time the victim may remain in the acute stage. The immediate symptoms may last a few days to a few weeks and may overlap with the outward adjustment stage.

According to Scarse there is no "typical" response amongst rape victims. However, the U.S. Rape Abuse and Incest National Network (RAINN) asserts that, in most cases, a rape victim's acute stage can be classified as one of three responses: expressed ("He or she may appear agitated or hysterical, [and] may suffer from crying spells or anxiety attacks"); controlled ("the survivor appears to be without emotion and acts as if 'nothing happened' and 'everything is fine'"); or shock/disbelief ("the survivor reacts with a strong sense of disorientation.

They may have difficulty concentrating, making decisions, or doing everyday tasks. They may also have poor recall of the assault"). Not all rape survivors show their emotions outwardly. Some may appear calm and unaffected by the assault.

Behaviors present in the acute stage can include:

- Diminished alertness.
- Numbness.
- Dulled sensory, affective and memory functions.
- Disorganized thought content.
- Vomiting.
- Nausea.
- Paralyzing anxiety.
- Pronounced internal tremor.
- Obsession to wash or clean themselves.
- Hysteria, confusion and crying.
- Bewilderment.
- Acute sensitivity to the reaction of other people.

The outward adjustment stage

Survivors in this stage seem to have resumed their normal lifestyle. However, they simultaneously suffer profound internal turmoil, which may manifest in a variety of ways as the survivor copes with the long-term trauma of a rape. In a 1976 paper, Burgess and Holmstrom note that all but 1 of their 92 subjects exhibited maladaptive coping mechanisms after a rape.

The outward adjustment stage may last from several months to many years after a rape.

RAINN identifies five main coping strategies during the outward adjustment phase:

- minimization (pretending 'everything is fine')
- dramatization (cannot stop talking about the assault)
- suppression (refuses to discuss the rape)
- explanation (analyzes what happened)
- flight (moves to a new home or city, alters appearance)

Other coping mechanisms that may appear during the outward adjustment phase include:

- poor health in general.
- continuing anxiety
- sense of helplessness
- hypervigilance
- inability to maintain previously close relationships
- experiencing a general response of nervousness known as the "startle response"
- persistent fear and or depression at much higher rates than the general population
- mood swings from relatively happy to depression or anger
- extreme anger and hostility (more typical of male or masculine victims than female or feminine victims)
- sleep disturbances such as vivid dreams and recurring nightmares
- insomnia, wakefulness, night terrors
- flashbacks
- dissociation (feeling like one is not attached to one's body)
- panic attacks
- reliance on coping mechanisms, some of which may be beneficial (e.g., philosophy and family support), and others that may ultimately be counterproductive (e.g., self-harm, drugs or alcohol abuse)

Lifestyle

Survivors in this stage can have their lifestyle affected in some of the following ways:

- Their sense of personal security or safety is damaged.
- They feel hesitant to enter new relationships.
- Questioning their sexual identity or sexual orientation (more typical of men raped by other men or women raped by other women.).
- Sexual relationships become disturbed. Many survivors have reported that they were unable to re-establish normal sexual relations and often shied away from sexual contact for some time after the rape. Some report inhibited sexual response and flashbacks to the rape during intercourse.
- Conversely, some rape survivors become hyper-sexual or promiscuous following sexual attacks, sometimes as a way to reassert a measure of control over their sexual relations.

Some rape survivors now see the world as a more threatening place to live after the rape so they will place restrictions on their lives so that normal activities will be interrupted. For example, they may discontinue previously active involvements in societies, groups or clubs, or a parent who was a survivor of rape may place restrictions on the freedom of their children.

Physiological responses

Whether or not they were injured during a sexual assault, rape survivors exhibit higher rates of poor health in the months and years after an assault, including acute somatoform disorders (physical symptoms with no identifiable cause). Physiological reactions such as tension headaches, fatigue, general feelings of soreness or localized pain in the chest, throat, arms, or legs.

Specific symptoms may occur that relate to the area of the body assaulted. Survivors of oral rape may have a variety of mouth and throat complaints, while survivors of vaginal or anal rape have physical reactions related to these areas.

Nature of the assault

- The nature of the act, the relationship with the offender, the type and amount of force used, and the circumstances of the assault all influence the impact of an assault on the victim.
- When the assault is committed by a stranger, fear seems to be the most difficult emotion to manage for many people. (Feelings of vulnerability arise).
- More commonly, assaults are committed by someone the victim knows and trusts. May be heightened feelings of self-blame and guilt.

Underground stage

- Victims attempt to return to their lives as if nothing happened.
- May block thoughts of the assault from their minds and may not want to talk about the incident or any of the related issues. (They don't want to think about it).
- Victims may have difficulty in concentrating and some depression.
- Dissociation and trying to get back to their lives before the assault.
- The underground stage may last for years and the victim seems as though that they are "over it", despite the fact the emotional issues are not resolved.

Reorganization stage

- May return to emotional turmoil

- The return of emotional pain can extremely frighten people in this stage.

- Fears and phobias may develop. They may be related specifically to the assailant or the circumstances or the attack or they may be much more generalized.

- Appetite disturbances such as nausea and vomiting. Rape survivors are also prone to developing anorexia nervosa and/or bulimia.

- Nightmares, night terrors feel like they plague the victim.

- Violent fantasies of revenge may also arise.

Phobias

A common psychological defense that is seen in rape survivors is the development of fears and phobias specific to the circumstances of the rape, for example:

- A fear of being in crowds.
- A fear of being left alone anywhere.
- A fear of men or women. (androphobia or gynophobia)
- A fear of going out at all, agoraphobia.
- A fear of being touched, hapnophobia.
- Specific fears related to certain characteristics of the assailant, e.g. side-burns, straight hair, the smell of alcohol or cigarettes, type of clothing or car.

- Some survivors develop very suspicious, paranoid feelings about strangers.
- Some feel a pervasive fear of most or all other people.

The renormalization stage

In this stage, the survivor begins to recognize his or her adjustment phase. Recognizing the impact of the rape for survivors who were in denial, and recognizing the secondary damage of any counterproductive coping tactics (e.g., recognizing that one's drug abuse began to help cope with the aftermath of a rape) is particularly important. Male victims typically do not seek psychotherapy for a long time after the sexual assault—according to Lacey and Roberts, less than half of male victims sought therapy within six months and the average interval between assault and therapy was 2.5 years; King and Woollett's study of over 100 male rape victims found that the mean interval between assault and therapy was 16.4 years.

During renormalization, survivors integrate the sexual assault into their lives so that the rape is no longer the central focus of their lives; negative feelings such as guilt and shame become resolved, and survivors no longer blame themselves for the attack.

Gun's

One day during coffee break, I was saying how my then wife was mad at me for buying a new security system. Someone asked me who made it and I said, "Mossberg." They said, "They make guns, don't they?" I replied, "Yes and it makes me feel more secure at home."

Before we go much further, let me just say how precious and irreplaceable every life is, even a thief's. Granted they may be lowlife pond scum but once you pull a trigger, you can never call the bullet back. Just like I used to tell my son, bullets are just like words. You can say you are sorry all you want, but once you let them go, there is just no calling them back. Enough said, but never put someone bent on taking your life above yourself.

Burglars and thieves can be divided into groups: the pro, the teenager, and the addict. I strongly suspect most teenagers will run at the mere site of a gun. I can personally attest to the fact that the addict will attack you. The pro is more likely to case out the premises and strike when no one is home. Believe it or not, most burglars are just trying to supplement their income. This is where an alarm system with cameras would come in real handy, especially if you ever expect to recover your property. I would like to remind you that a lot of rapes started out as a burglary.

Having walked in on a burglar, I have learned that they will use the dodge that they are looking for someone. But it did not work when I spied the forced door. While painting a house, two guys were wandering around and talking about the boat out back. When I approached them, one of them said he was looking for Chris. I got suspicious when he changed the name after I told him Chris was out back. I told the owner to make sure his insurance on the boat was paid up or sell it.

Many years ago, a then well-known comedian went to prison for setting himself on fire while smoking dope. I can remember when he got out he made jokes about his time in the pen. He was telling the audience how he asked one of his cellmates what he was in for and the guy said homicide. It ended with the comedian asking the guy why he killed the whole family. I can still remember and picture the comedian's expression when he mimicked the guy's response, "Cuz they was 'ome". This is no joke, there are people out there who will kill and have killed for the change in someone's pocket.

Be very sure that if you confront someone in your own home you are in grave danger. Especially if you are a woman. Be even more certain that the police will not get there in time to stop them. Make certain that it is more like they did not get there in time to stop you, if you know what I mean.

If you were to ask the experts about what type of gun to have, you would get many responses. Although I am no expert, I believe a shotgun with #2 birdshot is a good choice. It will stop someone that is close enough in your home but have a *smaller* chance of going through a wall and hitting a member of your own family. I am not a fan of 00 buck shot. Even with a long barrel it spreads out to quickly to have any real knock down power.

There is also a company that makes a fragmentation bullet called the Glaser Safety Slug.

BLUE: Glaser BLUE uses #12 shot compressed into a solid form. The Glaser BLUE immediately disperses energy into the target, reducing the possibility of over-penetration and creating abrupt stopping power. The numerous pellets disperse outward, generating an effective wound cavity.

SILVER: Glaser SILVER is made up of #6 shot. With the Silver load, you get much larger segments, deeper penetration and controlled energy release.

Both loads reduce the possibility of over-penetration through the intended target. They provide for an added margin of safety. A missed round is much more likely to break up on an interior wall and dump its energy rather than proceed unabated into an adjoining room. The light, fast bullets reduce the felt recoil, and are excellent loads for small compact carry guns and snub nose revolvers. For over 27 years, the Glaser Safety Slug has been the overwhelming choice for the "house gun" stored in the nightstand.

Having been in a fight with someone hopped up on drugs I can personally attest to the fact that hitting them between the legs three times with a club will have no effect whatsoever. Other than they will be real sore the next day. I do not recommend discharging mace inside your home since it will most certainly affect you as well.

The bad news with a gun is that in the dark you may accidentally shoot the wrong person. Next to your bed, always keep a flashlight. Get one with the button that you must push and hold. Use alkaline batteries so they will not corrode the flashlight. Also, do not use it for anything else. It will be dead when most needed. Do not use rechargeable batteries either. They do not give any advance warning that they are about to go dead. They will just plain go out, without the traditional gradual dimming of regular batteries. You can get ready made flashlights that can be attached to a gun barrel. Get one with a switch near the trigger so you can turn it on and off.

If you want some element of surprise on your side, buy night vision goggles. Always know what you are shooting at and keep your gun in a safe. Several under-the-bed safes exist that will hold a pistol just nice. Yes, I know I recommended a shotgun, but shotguns are not so easy to keep secure and readily available. Not to mention being hard to turn in close quarters. A short barrel will help compensate for that. Do not remove the stock and attach a pistol grip. It makes it too hard to aim accurately. If you are small framed opt for a 20-gauge shotgun as opposed to a 12 gauge. Pump action shotguns are much cheaper that a semi-auto and much more reliable, just don't buy a used one. My old used pump does not always chamber the round correctly.

If you have to shoot be below your target and shoot upward. Train your family members to lay prone on the floor when there is an intruder in your house. With friends and family on the floor this makes it harder to shoot one of them by accident. In close quarters things can and will happen fast, YOU BE FIRST. Always make two quick shots to the body.

Always identify your target that is what the flashlight or night vision goggles are for. When using a flashlight turn it on for just a second and do not be where you were when you light up the night. Which means just turn it on and off quickly to identify where you are while moving. Look ahead of you as far as you can see then lights out and go there. This works outside as well as inside. Always identify a place to retreat to also. Sometimes even go backwards. You are also illuminating your location while doing this which is why you need to make sure you do not stay where you were when your light was on.

Not to go on a rant, but every time an innocent member of the family is mistakenly shot or one gets hold of a loaded gun and shoots themselves or a playmate, the antis go on a bandwagon. An innocent person being shot is important so be responsible if you have guns and keep them locked in a safe. Given the price of a gun compared to safes now and that of a life, it is a small investment that will pay back many times its original cost.

I bought a gun safe not just because of my ex-wife's many threats to use one of my guns on me, but also because the peace of mind it gave me when we left home for days was well worth the investment.

One last thing, never lend a gun to anyone. I lent one to my brother and he lent it to one of his friends. I took it back before it went any further. Years later someone else asked to borrow one of my pistols. I refused, remembering my last mistake. Good thing – shortly thereafter he committed suicide.

When the trigger on a gun is pulled the firing, pin will impact the bullets primer. This will cause the primer to ignite causing the power inside the case to burn rapidly. The bullet has a wax ring at the base called lube. This provides a seal for the bullet as it is propelled down the barrel. The flash is the remaining un-burnt power. A rifle will have more energy for the same bullet as the barrel is longer compared to a pistol. So, a bullets velocity is affected by the barrel. Meaning two rifles with same barrel length and ammo will perform the same rather one is an assault weapon or not. Looking like an assault weapon does not change a thing either.

I don't recommend a rifle over a pistol for inside home defense. Never chose a 22 as a personal defense weapon. It uses a rim firing primer as opposed to center fire for all other primers. Too much chance of the primer not going off and it is not a big enough bullet.

I cannot recommend a specific gun for everyone. You will be the one who faces the consequences of your choice. Do your research thoroughly before you buy. I will give you some tips to aid you in the process though. As I've said never chose a 22 for personal defense. I don't advise buying used.

Too much is riding on your choice. Make sure you can control the gun. I witnessed one woman purchase a 44 magnum. Think Dirty Harry's gun. I don't care for magnums hand guns period. The bullet impacted way above the sights making hitting anything a total guess when I fired one.

I also do not favor revolvers. At best, they hold 6 rounds. Very few people hit 100% of the targets in a shootout; even the police. So, you should plan on reloading if you are not shaking too much. Semi-auto pistols hold clips that are easier to reload and have many more bullets in them. I don't favor 38's at all. A woman in Georgia shot an intruder 5 times with one and he walked away.

Find out the velocity and knock down power of a cartridge when shopping. If possible fire a gun like the one you are considering. Then practice with it afterwards. Handling a gun does not come naturally especially if you want to hit anything.

Always aim for the mass. If you are being shot at smaller targets are harder to hit; more so if they are moving.

Always be prepared to shoot if need be, otherwise don't pick up a gun. It could be taken away from you and used on you and other people afterwards. This is called "Failure to accept the consequences of your inaction". Need motivation; just think of what will happen to you if you don't shoot. Not going to get graphic but remember once you have been raped it lasts a life time. I have been accused of making too much of rape. I don't think so; there is only making too little of it. After just having read about its affects you should not either. Don't let it happen to you if at all possible. Best way to do that you ask? Buy a gun and learn how to use it.

In 1999, I was working in downtown Putnam Connecticut. One day about 10:20 a shot rang out. I yelled out for someone to lock the door saying, "That was a gunshot", which brought snickers. The next day I got apologies because the 6:00 news reported a murder in down town Putnam. As the facts came out it was a woman who had shot a man trying to rape her. She had stood there pointing a gun at him for 10 minutes and he did not get the message that she was not going to get raped. So, she shot him. Stalling, Pleading and reasoning with a rapist does not work and this is a perfect example. In the end, all she got was a year in prison for illegal possession of a hand gun. Remember this when you discover an intruder in your home or are attacked elsewhere. Sexual assault can happen anywhere any time. Sexual violence is also worldwide occurrence.

A female patient with a serious brain injury was raped at Bronx-Lebanon Hospital in New York on 9/4/2017. A nurse was checking on the 32-year-old patient when she walked in on 37-year-old Keith Nembhard having sex with the incapacitated woman. The victim's doctor said that the woman had a serious brain injury that rendered her incapable of consenting to sex. He was arrested and charged with rape in the second degree. Just goes to show that there is no limit to where and when this can happen.

Hearing through walls

Read the section on the laser where I explain how sound sets up vibrations in glass. Well it sets up vibrations in walls as well. Since I am not educating you on how to do these things, I will try to avoid the how-too. A contact microphone when placed against a door, wall or window will amplify the conversation within. Some are made to amplify voices by attaching directly to a person's neck. A contact microphone attached to a spike inserted into a wall and pressed up against but not through the opposite wall, will pick up the conversations in the target room. I found a near silent drill for drilling holes through walls just for this type of mic. It drills at slow speeds since that is what dictates the amount of noise as opposed to the material you are drilling through. Spike microphones can also be inserted through the cracks of doors and windows to pick up and amplify what is said inside. The Wireless Stethoscope Transmitter and Receiver Kit is designed to allow one to listen remotely through doors, windows and walls by utilizing up to 4 different stethoscope transmitters and can transmit the audio to a receiver up to 300 meters away. The frequency range of the transmitted signal is 800-2600 MHz. Not so lame now.

Ever notice when someone has spray-painted lines on the streets and sidewalks? Well, that is because they are tracing water pipes and wires. With water getting expensive today, many big cities have become concerned with leaks. So how can they hear through the ground? They do it pretty much like a doctor uses a stethoscope to hear your heart. Think a wall is so hard to hear through now? I found a device advertised as a wireless stethoscope transmitter that can be attached to doors walls and windows so the perp does not have to stand there to hear. Less chance of being caught.

Countermeasures. This is a tough one since microphones do not radiate a signal that can be tracked unless coupled to a transmitter. Best guess here is to open any electrical sockets on walls adjoining other apartments. Contractors are always taking the cheap way out, so often they will put electrical sockets back to back in adjoining apartments. Do you live in a duplex or apartment complex? Remember this when you stay in a hotel.

I was watching a *King Kong* movie in which the main character put a glass against a wall and his ear against the glass to hear what was being said in the next room. I promptly turned on my stereo and went out into the hall of my apartment. Guess what, it worked. I also know a woman who was arrested for doing that. Fortunately for her, the woman who caught her was doing the same thing. Which is how she caught her, so it was either they both went to jail or neither.

I found this little contact mic that you hold on to a wall and it will amplify the conversation in the next room. This is an active amplifier not passive like the glass. Meaning even if the people in the next room are talking in a low tone you simply turn up the volume. When mine arrived it worked, but also amplified the noise I made holding it. Very sensitive.

What Is Impersonation/Identity Fraud?

Impersonation fraud occurs when someone assumes your identity to perform a fraud or other criminal act. Criminals can get the information they need to assume your identity from a variety of sources, such as the theft of your wallet, your trash, or from credit or bank information. They may approach you in person, by telephone, or on the Internet and ask you for the information. Be cautious of the people you let into your home. Never use or enter your credit card info on a public computer network. Even your work internet access can be spied upon.

The sources of information about you are so numerous that you cannot prevent the theft of your identity. But you can minimize your risk of loss by following a few simple tips.

Some Tips to Avoid Impersonation/Identity Fraud:

- Never throw away ATM receipts, credit statements, credit cards, or bank statements in a usable form.
- Never give your credit card number over the telephone unless you have made the call.
- Reconcile your bank account monthly and notify your bank of discrepancies immediately.
- Keep a list of telephone numbers to call to report the loss or theft of your wallet, credit cards, etc.
- Report unauthorized financial transactions to your bank, credit card company, and the police, as soon as you detect them.
- Review a copy of your credit report at least once each year from the three major credit reporting agencies – Equifax, Experian and TransUnion – is easy and you're entitled to them under federal law. Notify the credit bureau in writing of any questionable entries and follow through until they are explained or removed.

- If your identity has been assumed, ask the credit bureau to print a statement to that effect in your credit report.
- If you know of anyone who receives mail from credit card companies or banks in the names of others, report it to local or federal law enforcement authorities.
- Be careful about whom you let into your home. Identity theft is often committed by friends or even relatives.
- Create a secure place to store all information about you that can be used to steal your ID, such as birth certificates and social security cards. Buy a safe for this purpose.

Password decoder software is available from numerous sources on the internet. When using your computer on the internet never click save your password or user name. Those so-called friends or relatives that commit identity theft can copy them and use this software to decrypt them. I learnt at a young age to never let thieves into my home, neither should you.

Some signs your identity has been stolen. 1 An increase in a credit balance. 2. Your credit card is declined. 3. Your credit score drops. 4. Unauthorized inquires on your credit score. 5. Mysterious new accounts. 6. Debt collectors are calling.

Your identity is your biggest asset, and your Social Security number is the key to your personal wealth. Also guard your birth date, driver's license number as well as credit card numbers. Since 2004 hackers and thieves have gained access to 600 million consumer files. Too many businesses ask for you SSN; that do not need it; just because they always have.

You can order and review your credit report online or request that a paper copy be sent to you in the mail. You can get your credit score for free every month on Credit.com. http://www.credit.com/credit-reports/free-annual-credit-report/ An unexpected change in your credit score from month to month can signal fraudulent activity.

About half of all identity theft is committed by close friends and relatives

Internet

Seventy percent of teens "hide their online behavior" from parents, according to a survey conducted by McAfee a software maker. This is up from 43% in 2010. From this survey 12% have met face to face with someone they have met on the internet. Parents can you say, "Key Logger". There is software out there made for parents and you need it because your kids are most likely to be more internet savvy than you are. I recommend filtering out Face book. I just read a story by a now 21-year-old female. She had fallen for the "I love you" line and met a man who friended her on Facebook. She said he dropped her off on a street corner first thing to prostitute herself for him. Which she did because he threatened to withhold his love from her. It was 3 years before she escaped. Don't be squeamish about eves dropping your children's internet activity. Especially if they close an internet window the minute you come in the room.

There have also been suicides from Face book as well. A young British girl committed suicide over naked pictures she had been conned into taking and sending to a man. He in turn posted them on FB and her whole school found out. Then he blackmailed her for more

Eighteen victims of child pornography were rescued during a nationwide sweep by federal law enforcement agencies. It was called Operation Orion, and resulted in the arrests of 190 individuals. "Many of the child exploitation cases under Operation Orion began with a child or teen chatting with someone he or she met online." as children begin summer vacations, parents should pay extra attention to how much time they spend on the Internet.

Many teens are on Facebook Twitter, Instagram, Tumblr, Vine and Pinterest. Kik, WhatsApp or Snapchat, can be used to send private messages to groups of friends. Snapchat also can be used to send nude pictures.

42 percent of teens have seen internet porn in the past year according to one study. Unfortunately, porn has become riddled with violence and contributes to the degrading of women. Repeated exposure to porn has chilling effects. Studies conducted in the 70's conclude that those exposed to large amounts of porn were more likely to condone violence against women even though the porn they viewed was nonviolent. You as a parent should regulate/monitor your child's internet activity; especially for girls. Talk to you children about porn and explain to them the degrading and violent influence it has on both sexes. Children are sexual creatures as well and will naturally develop curiosity about the other sex. Being open with them about sex is recommended and will immunize your child against porn if they can trust all of your answers. Install porn blockers on your computers as well as theirs. Porn can show up on screen rather intentional or accidental. Explain to your children that porn is not a real depiction of sex. Also discourage girls form participating in it.

The Internet is always changing and so are the scams people are using. Because of this, I am not going to try to cover everything, even were it humanly possible. But I am going to cover a few things anyways.

Do a search for your name. You will be surprised at the number of places where it will come up. Request that you be removed from them even if you are not female. I just found a URL of my name; it's not me but it was just a bit creepy.

It cost me nine dollars but I got information about myself and every other Daniel Hanson in my state. The nine dollars was just the start. Any juicier info would cost more. My point? Cover all the bases and ask to be removed. This is what they said: "The title, employment history, education and company data may provide useful professional information to help you locate an individual." For more money, I could find email address, reverse phone look up, addresses past and present and property values.

There is a software program called a Harvester. This program collects people's email address. This is why you will start to get spam the minute you open an email address, even one at Yahoo, Hotmail etc.

One reporter used a tool called Collusion to track who was tracking him; 105 companies tracked his Internet use during one 36-hour period.

Phishing attacks have seen a dramatic increase in recent years. Be careful when the economy is slowing the predators get desperate and very active. These will come to the potential victim disguised as an email from their credit card company, eBay, PayPal or any other names the criminals can find. However, the email is not from the stated business. It will claim you need to update or change your account info and send you to a bogus site disguised to look like the original. There you will be prompted to provide all the information the criminal needs to assume your identity and open your bank accounts. I got one just the other day claiming to be from the IRS and that they owed me $109 and I had to fill out a form to get it.

I was suspicious the minute it said the IRS owes me money. My second thought was, if they owe me, they know where to send it. Needless to say, I did not bite on that one. 30 million people were exposed to phishing and 3 per cent replied, providing information making them vulnerable.

Naturally, the real companies being impersonated are not happy to have their name dirtied by this and are actively helping track down the people behind these phishing attacks.

Some websites such as eBay or PayPal request that you forward this email to spoof@ebay.com or spoof@paypal.com. The similarity is not a coincidence. No matter what these emails say, do not click on them and provide the requested information. Forward the email to any entity that is being impersonated and to spam@uce.gov.

Imposter schemes involve some one posing as a friend or relative in need of help either on line or on the phone. Always verify the situation by contacting other friends or family. After all, if you can't trust family who can you trust today? This is one of the fasted growing scams, sadly because it works. They average 3 to 4 thousand dollars.

Then there is the Nigeria scam. This will come as an email from someone who introduces themselves as the wife, son etc. of some late important so and so. They want your help collecting their inheritance or want to donate money etc.

Basically, this will lead to you having to give them your personal info so they can make this deposit or they want some security from you. Do not even reply to these. Some people have gone to Nigeria because of these and ended up dead. Needless to say, the Nigerian government will not be sympathetic since you were trying to steal its money.

I know someone from Nigeria who was telling me about an incident where a white man went wandering around town and was kidnapped and had his privileges (as he described them) cut off. Does not sound like a place I will be going to any time soon.

Only 1 in 42 work at home schemes are legit. If the pay is too good to be true it is a scam also if you are asked to pay to join. Kiss that money good bye.

When purchasing anything online, when you get to the order page, look at the URL heading. If it does not begin with *https*, it is not a secure transaction. The S stands for secure.

Then there was the bug in the open-source Open SSL cryptography library, which is widely used to implement the Internet's Transport Layer Security (TLS) protocol.

Be wary of people who are around you when entering a pass word; especially if they are always there when you are typing. Examine your keyboard for any light power.

Beware of the stranded friend or hardship plea for funds for relative's surgery. Face book accounts have been hacked and friends have been duped only to find out that their friends were not away from home. There are so many variations on this; just do not fall for them.

It is a check scam when a check arrives for more that the amount for what you may have sold online. Then the thief will request you to send back the overage. By the time you find out the original check was bad they have your money and item. Always use PayPal and if locally meet in a public place and deal only in cash.

R.A.T. Remote Access Tools AKA Ratters.

This software that gets on your computer by social engineering is similar to the software used by IT depts. for tech support. Only this is used by hackers to gain access to your computer its info and or your web cam. Unsuspecting women are being watched unaware and their video is being posted on YouTube.

Some images taken from the "Slaves" hard drive are also appearing on the internet. These Ratters can scare and annoy their victims. The can open and close DVD drives. Have your computer talk using text to speech programs. Posting images of their choosing on screen. Microphones and cameras can be remotely turned on, on smartphones laptops and tablets to eavesdrop on the owner.

Infection is done the same way any virus can get onto your computer. If you see that your web camera light is on and you are not using it run antivirus sw. Stay safe by using a firewall regularly run antivirus software and stay away from sketchy web sites and torrent sites. Ratter's seed files on these sites disguised as free videos, music or software programs.

Change the default passwords when you receive your web camera to something other than the default. Also change the port used.

Forums are growing where these raters can talk about their exploits. This means it is growing in popularity and a woman needs to be careful. One never knows when you may have a stalker until too late.

New TVs feature video cameras and microphones. The privacy policy on a web based TV states "Do not say or do anything of a personal nature near the TV, even if it is not on." Best solution is to unplug it if you absolutely needed to buy one in the first place. Believe anything to do with the web can be hacked.

Despite any claims to the contrary I have never trusted the cloud to be absolutely secure. It came as no surprise to me when famous female actors had their nude pictures hacked from the cloud and publicized. Best advice the net and naked pictures don't go together. Come to think of it exactly what do you need naked pictures for?

Software exists that can hack a person's cell phone to listen in on and track its location using GPS

MLM marketing is where you get two that get two etc. This is just another form of the pyramid scam. The only ones making the money are the ones starting these. There is always someone on the bottom paying someone above. When they run out of new people coming in at the bottom, the scheme will collapse, just like the never-ending pyramid scams.

Be wary of limited time offers. They will come and go real fast. Never to be seen or heard from again. Forget about all these free grants. The only ones that are qualified are non-profit organizations. Save your money.

In the end, the only victim of unauthorized use of someone's credit card is the vendor. Not the bank or cardholder. That does not make it right. You the cardholder always have the right to dispute a charge. Make sure you do it immediately, even if the thief is using it less than your wife. Never leave any credit card charge slips around. Destroy them before disposing of them. Buy yourself a paper shredder one that also cross cuts.

IR Microphone Transmitter

These little devices will transmit the audio in a room via infrared light. They also require a special receiver, which eliminates normal receivers and detection. They can work up to a range of 500 meters and requires a line of sight. A window is the only means for these to transmit to the receiver. Look very closely at any items next to your windows – plants, pots, the curtains, anything close to a window – if you suspect their use. One model can be attached to the outside of a window and pick up conversations. So, clean your windows often.

Countermeasures. Close your blinds. Buy some if you don't have any. Make sure nothing has been attached to them. As mentioned before, you can check for this with night vision goggles. A IR camera would work as well. During the day might it might be difficult detect. I suspect this may be a little harder to detect with night vision goggles and would suggest using some sort of dust or powder to help illuminate the beam. Use it outside so you don't have to worry about a mess.

Extreme, probably, but remember this is about how, not if, someone is watching you. A Google search for these IR transmitters revealed many that are not meant for concealment. It should come as no surprise then that all that needs to be done is make one small enough to avoid detection by the victims.

The pros always get hold of the latest and greatest before the general population. Actually, what I see being offered to the public is really lame. I have no doubt that this is deliberate. Some firms are advertising their products as police grade.

LASER Listening Device

This laser listening device is used to listen to conversation inside a room without ever having to break and enter to place an electronic bug. It can also be located as far as a mile away from the target's window. Lasers have been used since the 1960s for spying. Having seen one of these available at a show, I can tell you that they are not just used by the government anymore.

This is a very expensive piece of equipment, not to mention the fact that invasion of privacy is a five-year prison sentence. It stands to reason that if someone is willing to take this risk, then they have more than just listening to your conversations in mind. Especially if caught, it could mean five years of their lives in the big house (Leavenworth). If someone is spending thousands of dollars on this equipment; you better believe they are going to use it.

Two weaknesses of this device are that it requires a 90-degree angle to the subject's window and a visible light is needed to perform the alignment. So, if you are watching TV and a red dot appears on your wall, you now know why.

Laser is an acronym that means Light Amplification by Stimulated Emission of Radiation. I hated physics in college, but I did learn something that will help you the reader to understand why this is worth telling you about. So here goes. Believe it or not but every color you see has its own specific frequency. Some of you might remember seeing a color chart on the wall of the chemistry department. Our sun, the greatest illuminator around, generates every frequency in the color spectrum and then some. Such as ultraviolet and infrared light along with visible light. With each color having its own frequency range. So, you ask why we can see only one color at a time. When light hits an object, it is either reflected or absorbed. Since light is a form of energy, if it is absorbed it converts to heat.

Now back to the color chart – white on the far left tends to reflect more light and black on the right end tends to absorb all lesser frequencies Now if you are wearing black you will be hotter than you know what in July. This is also why people in the tropics wear white and bright flowery shirts. So, don't wear black unless you happen to be in the Antarctic and want to be as hot as you can, or do not want to show up at night. Black pajamas are good for some things, but don't go jogging in them at night; you might end up as road kill.

Stay with me, folks, its all, relative. Lasers have a unique characteristic in that they are monochromatic and coherent. Mono means "one" which means that a laser has just one frequency of light at all times. At all times means coherent. To be more specific, if you could look at the light coming out of the laser sideways, it would be the same frequency everywhere at once. This frequency is in the nanometers range (1319 or 1064) and is very precise. Some Einstein figured out that if he took a laser beam and pointed it at a moving car and then did some math with the returning beam, he could come up with the car's speed. Now we have new-fangled radar for getting money out of speeders. This laser is in the infrared region, which is why you never see it coming.

Most inventions have come about in answer to a recognized need. Necessity is the mother of invention. A unique fact about the laser is that it was an invention in search of a need. Unfortunately, sooner or later someone's thoughts always turn towards evil. Before Cain killed Abel, who would have thought you could have done that with a rock? Now everybody knows.

Another not so useless fact that figures into this equation is that glass is a liquid. No, I am not off my rocker; glass really is a liquid. The moment it is suspended vertically, it starts to flow downwards. Remember seeing an old building with windows that had lines in the glass and things appear a little distorted through them?

This is a result of this flow over time, a very long time. If you were to remove a pane and measure the thickness at the top and bottom, you would find the bottom thicker. Since glass is a fluid, as you speak in a room it will move in reaction to your sound waves, although not very much which is why a laser in the nanometers range is required.

Some Einstein figured out that if you took a laser, aimed it at the window of a room and did some magic number crunching on the returning signal, you could hear what was being said in the room. See, I told you it was all relative. This was done long before laser radar came along, which probably made figuring out the radar easy.

There is a lot more involved than what I have told you. This infrared laser microphone is not something anyone can whip up in his or her garage. I did not come up with this but had to hear about it somewhere else; just like I said, men's hearts have turned to evil before. I am not telling anyone who wants to do this something they don't already know. I am telling you this so you will be aware of what people can do to you.

I did some research on the Web to determine how laser radar worked. I was curious as to how a narrow beam of light could possibly be reflected back to a small device from a moving car. It turns out that the beam is spread out to the point that it covers the whole car. Lenses can be used to diverge or converge the beam. I have often wondered how difficult it would be to convert the laser radar to a listening device.

I recently read in a very well know magazine that these are far more effective than even I realized. Not going to tell how but you want to be very aware of these. Some are coming with the transmitter and receiver implanted in a camera so you would never guess you are being spied on you should you actually see it.

Then of course there is always tape recorders or digital recorders so it does not have to be babysat. Factor in voice activation and this could be left alone a long time.

Counter measures

You can check for infrared light beams with some night vision scopes. Smoke could be used to aid in detection. Laser light does not travel like the beams that are depicted on television. You can see the source and the destination but unless something like dust or smoke passes through the beam, you will not see it along its path. If you have seen a laser pointer then you have seen proof of this. The dot on the window can be detected with night vision goggles since they operate in the infrared range, unless of course the snoop at the source sees you and turns them off. Also, an inferred camera can detect the dot as well. I purchased a Minolta Dimage 7 and could see my ir laser quite well. Problem is this camera has not been made since 1999, but they are cheap. I bought mine for about $50. It must be the Dimage 7 not the 7i.

A laser radar detector does not detect all laser light signals. One difficult part is that the laser radar's beam is deliberately diverged to spread out, whereas the laser bug is focused into a single thin beam of light. Which could prove to be like trying to find a needle in a haystack. This is also why a 90-degree angle with the window is required. Any difference in the angle and the returning reflected beam would miss the laser receiver circuitry completely.

Do a search on the Internet for IR photo detectors. Stay within the wavelength of infrared light, which is 0.7 micrometers, extending to 300 micrometers. The infrared portion of the electromagnetic spectrum is usually divided into three regions: near-, mid- and far- infrared, named for their relation to the visible spectrum (Wikipedia).

Do a search on the web for "Laser Surveillance Defeater" to find another countermeasure device. This will foil the snoop by transmitting the frequencies of the human voice to the window to which it is attached. No word on how loud this is. This is to make the window glass vibrate out of synch with your conversation. Making the notch filter at the receiving portion of the laser bug produce some unintelligible noise. This will run for 500 hours on one battery, has an on/off switch and a bright blue power indicator. It attaches to the window via the suction cup. Unfortunately, it will only protect one window. Also, it is $79.95 as of this writing.

Also do an internet search for "High-performance Infrared Pulse 3 Beams Detector". Also called Security Alarm 2 Beam IR Detector can also be found as 3 and possible 4 beam. I purchased a 2 beam and pointed my infrared lasers the receiver and it detected them. Problem is the laser has to be pointed right at the lenses. It also requires an external 12 or 24VDC supply. So you will have to have a long power supply and wave it around on the inside of each window without missing a spot to work. Good news is this will work in daylight where the Minolta Dimage is not so good at ir in the daytime.

Mail

Just how safe is your mail? Not very, if someone wants to look at it. There are two chemicals that anyone can buy that, sprayed on your mail, will make the envelope transparent and will dry without a trace. There is also a chemical that will dissolve the glue on an envelope, allowing it to be opened, read and resealed without the owner being any the wiser. Note that I am not telling what they are since I am only educating you the reader on what can be done to you, not how to do it to someone else.

I once had an in-law whose mail never arrived on time, and when it did, it had all been opened. Even though they had a strong indication of who was doing it, they could not get any legal action. Don't dwell on it, but the only thing they could do was get a PO Box. If you are a woman who lives alone or has people who may be too curious about you, then I suggest the same. Of course, if you find you have too many people asking you if you got their letter, and you never did, then you also have a problem. If you ever want to catch a predator in the act, here is a good application for a hidden camera.

To keep the idle curious peeping Tom from reading your mail, use aluminum foil to prevent anything from being sprayed on it. The addresses that your mail comes from will also reveal a lot about you; another good reason to get a PO Box if you think you have nosey neighbors.

Forwarding addresses are a matter of public record and can be obtained both legally and falsely. If you have to move and really do not want certain people to be able to find you, I suggest paying all your bills and not leaving a forwarding address. Bill collectors can gain access to your new address by various means and find you for someone. Do not leave any legal reason behind for someone to locate you, so pay all your bills before leaving town. Especially if you have been a crime victim and someone might be looking for revenge.

Yes, I know of an instance where that happened. After buying a house, it has surprised me how many companies have been able to find me. Thanks to the Internet.

Now for some sever paranoia. You can put some Kool Aid crystals in your envelope. Use some photo glue just inside the flap. If and when it is steamed open, the crystals will dissolve and stain the contents. However, it may never reach its intended address. Or use carbon paper or graphite tracing paper to reveal any tampering. Lastly look at the edge for a small razor thin cut. A little ingenuity and dexterity and a letter can be removed through that small cut then reinserted.

Miscellaneous

DNR Dialed Number Recorder. This is used to record the number called from a targeted phone. Also used by hotels to keep track of your phone bill. I bought one for $50. It records all outgoing calls, but to record incoming calls you need caller ID.

If you ever want to assess a person's intelligence, look at their vocabulary. Why would you want to know this? Say you are a supervisor interviewing someone. Or better yet, maybe you are considering marrying someone. This is a good time to make sure you are equally yoked.

If your phone rings and there is no answer to your "Hello" right off, hang up quickly, it is a telemarketer. I was at a friend's house when his wife answered the phone and said that there was no one there. I said, "Hang up quickly, it's a telemarketer." To which the person calling asked, "How did he know that?"

Swimming. If in a foreign country you see a swimming hole with a *No Swimming* sign, don't go in. A television documentary interviewed a couple that did just that and the husband almost died from the infection he got. Foreign countries do not have the environmental laws that we do and most anything can and does end up in the water. Like fecal matter.

Closer to home, we have a flesh-eating bacterium that has killed a few people. They found out that it is caught by going into the water with open wounds from accidents or surgery. This bacterium is lurking in the pond pudding on the bottom and in the oceans. I remember watching the news with a doctor examining a patient. You could literally see the flesh disappear. You just can't live without your skin. You will die from a massive infection. The doctor even touched the affected area to demonstrate that you could not catch it by contact.

In my teen years, I remember seeing an advertisement for those funny-looking glasses that it was claimed could make you see through people's clothes. While in the Air Force, one day I was in the day room and there was a guy on TV wearing these glasses ogling a woman. I asked one of the other guys if they really worked. He said they did. Well, since this is about what can be done to you, I did a search for seeing through clothes. I found an IR filter that can be attached to the front of a camera lens that can indeed see through clothes. I'll let you know how well it works. That is a joke, folks. There are plenty of strip joints where I can see everything for small change.

If you are in a mall or any public place, beware of anyone with a camera with a brown filter attached to their camera. The manufacturer of this filter also had a gelatin version that could be cut down and taped over cell phone lenses.

This works because infrared light easily passes through a medium because of its long wavelength. The object behind it; say a person; will then reflect it back. A CCD (Charge Coupled Device) converts the infrared into a visible image. It can also be used to see through ink as well as clothes. I am getting one to test its ability to detect infrared lasers. Some of the landscape pictures looked really good too.

I have read about naked pictures of women appearing on porn sites on the Internet without their knowledge. There are perverts out there galore.

Be very suspicious of a financial deal/investment that seems too good to be true. It usually is. If it is an all or nothing opportunity opt for the nothing. The con artists want to leave you with nothing so you do not have the wherewith all to pursue them. Don't fool yourself; law enforcement will not have the burning desire to pursue them and very seldom do they ever recover anyone's money.

Do an internet search for "Tactical Pen" they feature a sharp and strong crown that can be used to attach a rapist and also will collect DNA.

Always keep your keys in your possession. If your car goes in the garage give just the ignition key. I have seen a gas station attendant make an impression of a customer's key. Keep any gas cap keys on a separate detachable loop. Watch your credit card transactions closely. There is a small device the size of a pack of cigarettes that your card info can be gotten just by swiping it. Also, be very observant when using an ATM card. Criminals place a device over the ATM slot that looks just like one. When you insert your card, it collects the info they need to create a duplicate and with the little camera they also plant they get your pin number. This tech has existed for decades and only gotten better. Put your hand over the slot and if it wiggles notify the bank and do not use it. Also, always place your hand over the keypad when entering your number.

When you travel beware of pizza flyers. Do not order from them using a CC. While you wait for your pizza the thieves are ordering things with it.

Texting abbreviations parents should be aware of

1. **IWSN** - I want sex now, 2. **GNOC** - Get naked on camera, 3. **NIFOC** - Naked in front of computer, 4. **PIR** - Parent in room, 5 **CU46** - See you for sex, 6. **53X** – Sex, 7. **9** - Parent watching, 8. **99** - Parent gone. 9 **1174'** - Party meeting place, 10. **THOT** - That hoe over there, 11. **CID** - Acid (the drug), 12. **Broken** – Hung over from alcohol, 13. **420** – Marijuana, 14. **POS** - Parent over shoulder, 15. **SUGARPIC** - Suggestive or erotic photo, 16. **KOTL** - Kiss on the lips, 17. **(L)MIRL** - Let's meet in real life, 18. **PRON** – Porn, 19. **TDTM** - Talk dirty to me 20. **8** - Oral sex, 21. **CD9** - Parents around/Code 9, 22. **IPN** - I'm posting naked, 23. **LH6** - Let's have sex, 24. **WTTP** - Want to trade pictures?, 25. **DOC** - Drug of choice, 26. **TWD** - Texting while driving, 27. **GYPO** - Get your pants off, 28. **KPC**- Keeping parents clueless.

If you are abducted and your hands are duck taped together use a shoelace as a saw which cuts through the tape quickly and easily. If zip ties are used to bind you, get your hands out from behind your back, hold them straight out in front of you and then pull them back, elbows at your side. You will have to be very limber to get your hands out from behind you but you can do it.

Do not read romance novels. Rape or near-rape fantasies are central to romance novels, one of the perennial best-selling categories in fiction. Romance novels are often called "porn for women." Porn is all about sexual fantasies. In porn for men, the fantasy is sexual abundance--eager women who can't get enough and have no interest in a relationship. In porn for women as depicted in romance novels, the fantasy is to be desired so much that the man loses all control. Gleaned from Psychology Today written by Michael Castleman M.A posted Jan 14 2010.

Even though you do not want to be assaulted it will make you do things that will increase the likely hood of it happening to you. Trust me on this; I have witnessed several examples of this.

On August 23, 2017, the FDA recalled 465,000, RF-enabled pacemakers to reduce the risk of patient harm due to potential exploitation of cybersecurity vulnerabilities. (Hacking) There are no known reports of patients being harmed relating to the cybersecurity vulnerabilities in the implanted devices. This should educate you on the vulnerability of today's technology.

Nothing Held Back

I have decided to include this chapter to emphasize how important this material is. I cannot overestimate how important it is to take my material seriously. There are rapists out there and there are a lot of companies making money selling spy equipment. So how does spy equipment help a rapist? First thing that comes to mind is they will be able to tell when you are home alone; or where you are going that they can ambush you at. Remember rape is a control thing not a crime of passion. Be wary of people who say you or they cannot do something that clearly can be done.

When I was about 12 my mother and step father were talking about a guy that was drunk. He was bragging about the sexual assaults he had committed. I got a piece of paper and pen and asked them to repeat the dates and address he had given. Then I called the police in both towns and asked them if they had a reported assault on this date at this address. When they said yes; I gave them his name.

I knew a couple who took in state kids. One girl was raped by her uncle right in her driveway. They almost believed her uncle until I pointed out that she had nightmares. One girl was taken from her mother along with her sister. The mother had brought five guys home from a bar. They got tired of waiting their turn with the mother and decided to help themselves to both her daughters as well. And the mother never did a thing to stop them.

Before getting my driver's license, I was hitchhiking and got picked up by a man and his wife. Do not do that today. As we drove by a factory they told me that their daughter had been kidnapped by three men from a convenience store and driven there and gang raped. I can still remember them telling me how her boyfriend cried. Later they realized their mistake and I ended up at the police station where I meet the daughter.

Naturally she wanted me not to tell anyone. One way to solve a rape is to ask the right questions. It turns out that her parents had sent her to that store at 1:30 in the morning for soda. Now for the details. This was in a small town in Maine when nothing would ever be open at that time. Did I mention that this was a long time ago? I asked her; what was the first thing her parents did when she got home. She said, "Gave me soda".

Then I asked if they were involved with the occult. She said they were. Then I asked if they had made any increases in the ranks and she said they had. Then I asked if that happened after her rape. That was when she started crying.

Find that hard to believe? Very pregnant Fernanda Pereyra, 26 was stabbed to death and burned to ashes in a suspected satanic ritual, police say. She, was barbarically killed before her body was burned in a fire so hot, she could only be identified by her necklace. Police have arrested three people in connection with the killing: her former boyfriend Luciano Hernandez and his two friends Osvaldo Castillo and Diego Marillan. They have also been linked with drug trafficking and are thought to practice Satanism.

In the 90's I was out of work a lot and while searching for a job remember being in a building with a small business on the right of the hall as you step inside. It had glass facing the lobby with two women working there. I remember a blond woman coming in with a picnic basket. She approached the two women who worked there and asked them if they would deliver the basked to her husband on the seventh floor who was doing construction. She claimed it was to be a surprise.

Knowing what I know I had doubts so I volunteered to do it. She refused my offer and left. Knowing that her husband and friend were still upstairs I went into the business the woman worked at and picked up the phone to call the police. Just as I heard the dispatcher the phone went dead.

One of the women had pulled the wires to the phone out. I don't remember the exact order but the phone company though I should pay for the repair. I believe they had to go to the police to identify me.

Anyways I found out that the woman with the basket came back but this time the two women took it up stairs. Some people are just so gullible. Evidently the woman with the basket though so and came back again with the same routine a second time. Only this time the police were waiting. I remember them telling me they caught the wife outside using a radio to tell her husband "they fell for it again". Wish I could have seen their faces when the elevator opened and there stood the police and not the intended victims.

I can still remember my ex-wife being questioned by her female coworkers what she would do if she was raped. Her answer of "If I get raped and don't tell I get divorced" saved her from being raped. I cannot say it enough never ever tell anyone you could never go through a rape trial.

I was in Vermont and there was a detailed article in the local paper of a 16-year-old that had raped a 71-year-old woman. The details that I remember are that he had stalked her. Three days before the rape he had come to her house and knocked on the door asking for a glass of water. I don't think that was a crime of passion. I am not looking forward to 70-year old's even when I get to be 70.

I cannot over state that rape can happen anywhere at any time. The sooner you realize this; the better your chances of avoiding it. If you run around believing it could not happen to you the more likely you are to be victimized. That is called naive. The type rapists look for. So how is this for a reflection on society?

In October 2009, a 15-year-old female student at Richmond High School in San Francisco was gang raped for over two and a half hours at a school dance. The victim was flown from the scene in critical condition after being raped by four suspects. Investigators stated that as many as 15 people stood around watching but did not call police.

Very few women actually escape their rapist, studies show that fighting back can increase the likelihood of escaping rape. So; you are a very lucky person if you do escape.

With DNA, today they very well could be identified in other rapes. States are required by law to do DNA tests on everyone arrested. Did I mention that rapists have on average 25 victims?

Report every attempted rape. I have only testified during two rape trials. During the first I was asked why the rapists had done one particular thing and my response was "Someone escaped" If that woman had reported the attempted rape perhaps this last victim may not have been raped. They got 45 years and are to my knowledge still in jail.

Given that 80% of rapists are known by their victims or if you are being stalked not reporting an attempted rape will be interpreted by your attacker as a green light that he can get away with the big event. I met a woman in a park who told me she was being stalked by some guy. I asked her if she had gone to the police. She said she did not because he had not said anything to her. I told her and say to you the laws no longer require a stalker to say anything to be prosecuted. Report every attempted rape. This is just a test; can I get away with raping you? Same if some guy gets tacky with you. Beware of men who do not interact to well with woman. In a genuine attack over react. A guy asking you out on a date is not the same thing. Beware if he says he only wants one date.

Quoted from a CCN article" **Why fraternities should admit women"** Sept 2014 by *Nicholas L. Syrett is associate professor of history at the University of Northern Colorado and the* *author of "The Company He Keeps: A History of White College Fraternities* "Men rape women because they believe they are entitled and because they think they can get away with it". Yah go ahead and not report an attempted rape. Syrett seems to think that admitting women to fraternities would lessen the number of college rapes because somehow the fraternity men will now view the women as sisters. I disagree. Teaching men that they are somebody's sister may help but giving them easy access to their victims is not going to help in my opinion.

I cannot overstate the importance to report every attempted rape or threat to do so. Sometime during the 1980 there was an article in the Worcester Telegram about a gruesome murder.

I went to the public library to look through the microfilm to find it but just made myself sick watching all the print go by while searching. Do not contact them to verify this story they do not keep records this far back.

This is a story of a couple who had 3 children and a friend named Angel. The parents and the friend Angel were out to a club or restraint together. Angle demanded sex from the woman and stated that if she did not have sex with him he would go to their house and stab their children to death. She/they did not take him seriously like they should have.

Only one child survived. I can remember the newspaper article stating that a cigarette lighter that turned out to belong to Angel was found in the home.

In March of 1983 a woman was gang raped on a pool table in a bar named Big Dan's Tavern in New Bedford Massachusetts. The significant and sick thing about this rape that makes it deserve mention is that no one in the bar intervened while some cheered them on. Six men were originally charged but two were acquitted. The victim was just 21 and died in a car accident at the age of 25.

Phones

A device exists that uses the unused pair of wires on your own phone lines. The yellow and black wires can be used to transmit your audio. I strongly suggest that you cut these wires before they exit your home to prevent any misuse of them. This device works by placing a microphone in your home at any phone jack in the room. The receiver can be placed miles away with a voice-operated tape recorder. The power supply is also at the receiver. I also suggest taking your phone apart and looking for any mics. Also, check the junction boxes.

If you live in an apartment building, your phone line can be tapped into by, say, a nosey landlord. Another extension can be simply attached to your line by anyone who has access to the lines. Inspect them regularly if you can. I have a sister who told me that she could hear her landlord's phone ring every time hers did, and stop when she picked up. She moved.

I found this on a web site.

Simple electronic circuit lets you pick up any extension phone without the users hearing a click. Great for checking on unauthorized phone use. Also, would work with the Hook Switch bypass.

I am not telling you where to find these devices. I remember a seventeen-year-old that was caught doing this and no it was not me. This was a long time ago and I am sure there are more devices out in society today. Also, be aware that they are far more sophisticated today.

Even if you have no reason to believe that you may be bugged, the people living there before you may have been and I firmly believe most people who place a bug will not risk being caught removing it.

They have gotten very cheap and always have been when compared to prison time. If sweeping for bugs, it will be necessary to use your phone to make these taps give off their presence. A tap can also be installed on your phone line a very long distance from your home. There are plenty of junction boxes that can be accessed. You can see them outside of office buildings and housing complexes. They are not always large either.

Then of course there is the legal kind. Sorry to mention this but temptation is just too much. Presently the police can legally quote randomly unquote listen to people's phone conversations. Given their success rate, one has to wonder just how random such listening really is. With the new terrorist laws enacted post 9/11, law enforcement now has a more general approach to monitoring a suspect. One wiretap authorization will blanket cover all of the target's communication methods. Home, cell, pager, fax and email etc.

Business phones are the property of the business and you as an employee do not have the right to a private conversation on these phones. Your conversation can be legally monitored and recorded. Believe me, high-tech companies have a vested interest in whether their employees are selling company secrets. Having worked in the high-tech sector, I remember seeing a guy come in and out of the telephone room as if he lived there. The companies also keep track of the numbers called as well. This is not just for the high-tech companies. So next time you are talking mushy to your sweaty etc., know that you may not be alone. The same applies to any emails you use through your company.

One phone tap, called the XXXXX Device, draws its power off the phone lines and transmits the audio off the lines. This device is activated by calling the target on the phone and whistling (Older models) the instant they hang up.

Today they can be activated by simply pressing a number on a digital phone before the target phone even rings. If this does not work and they answer the predator will simply say "Sorry wrong number". Fact or fiction but I believe this was used during Nam, but this time when they whistled the phone blew up.

It is possible for the operator or someone else to listen down your phone line and hear inside your residence even when the phone is resting in its cradle using a Hook switch bypass also known as an XXXXX Transmitter. Once activated the target phone can be monitored and recorded anywhere in the world from a phone. It is called the XXXXXX transmitter because of the unlimited range this gives it. Fortunately, it requires an internal modification to you phone or it can be attached directly to the line.

You can detect tampering to your phone by applying something called torc seal or just use plain white out like I did to the screws holding my phone together. Add some paint to tint it so that a predator cannot simply redo it.

A new spin on this is called a GSM SIM Card Surveillance Spy Bug. Just like the name says it uses a SIM card to accomplish the same thing. Drawbacks are that you have to buy a SIM card with the monthly fee and they only run for about 4 hours on a single charge.

One way to use these for your defense is to install one in your car or home. Then when you are in a mall or etc. it can call you if an intruder breaks into your car or home.

Kits that can be used to tap a phone are very common and easy to obtain. A nosey person can place a phone tap way down the phone line, anywhere between the target's home and the central phone company. This eliminates the necessity to break and enter. Some of these work by sensing the voltage on the line.

And when it drops, a relay closes, starting a recorder or transmitter. Some countermeasure devices maintain the line voltage when the phone is in use, preventing the relay from tripping.

There are methods for discovering a tap. Unfortunately, there is also a tap device that cannot be detected by these methods. Every line with electricity flowing through it radiates an electromagnetic field around the wire. This field can be picked up and amplified using a XXXX connected to the phone wire. Having no drain and leaving no trace on the taped line. The common television amplifies the signal received at the antenna one million times, so trust me when I say the field around a telephone wire can be amplified.

Another example of this electric field is called cross talk. Every so often when you are on the phone, you can hear a faint part of another phone conversation. I even managed to get a tip about a job this way. This happens because the phone wires are in close proximity in the cables and lie within each other's electromagnetic fields.

Mobil phones and some answering machines can be hacked also. In 2011 the British tabloid "The News of the World" closed after a lengthy investigation into the illegal phone hacking done by its reporters. They had used simple techniques to eves drop on the royal family and even the family of a teenage murder victim along with anybody they considered newsworthy.

Should you ever be targeted your mobile phone will be first choice of hackers/stalkers seeking sensitive info about you.

Change the default pass code to your voicemail and answering machine if it has one. Do it now if you have not already done so. When setting up voicemail the pass codes are always defaulted to a simple set of digits. Not saying what they may be.

Whenever you create a voicemail account learn how to change the pass code.

Do this for answering machines if you can remotely retrieve your message. Ask the store employee to show you how but do not give them your new pass code.

Call your wireless company and set additional levels of conformation. Without this a simple call to your phone carriers by a hacker could have your codes reset to an easy to guess default again. The personal information info the carrier will request to gain access to your account is easier to obtain than your code itself.

Keep your phone locked at all times the new smart phones are at risk when they are lost or stolen and fall into the wrong hands. Built in apps allow you to check new messages with just a touch.

Pick a hard to guess code the best will hold no significance to you at all. Random meaningless codes are key.

Never use:

Numbers in sequence (1234)

Dates, years ect. IE your birthdate.

Repeating numbers (6666)

Spelling and words.

Social Security numbers or parts.

Cell phones can also be tapped into. I distinctly remember a few years ago a television news show on how it was possible to buy a black box that captured people's info, allowing thieves to mimic a victim's phone, sticking them with the bill. Be aware that on these phones you may not be a two-party only conversation.

A company called Armis has found eight exploits, they call Blueborne, that can allow access to your phone without touching it. They can also allow access to both computers and phones as well as IoT devices. Blueborne can hack pretty much every device we use via Bluetooth. This attack does not require any user interaction, authentication or pairing, making it practically invisible. How do you stay safe? Keep all of your devices updated regularly and be wary of older IoT devices. Patches will eventually fix weakness as they are reported. Remember heartbleed that forced many web servers to display passwords and other keys remotely.

Drones have been equipped with technology that can steal your info on your smart phone. The research done will be presented at a Black Hat conference. In one hour of flight time researchers were able to obtain GPS locations on 150 people. This also can collect user names passwords and credit card numbers. You can protect yourselves by shutting off Wi-Fi connections and forcing your smart phone to ask before connecting.

There are cell phone jammers that can prevent you from calling for help. The ones I see available only work out to 10 meters; lame. I can't see one legal use even for the police. What are they trying to do, keep you from calling the police? Look for a hand-held device with 3 antennas. One device can locate a cell phone when it is in range even if the phone is not being used (standby mode) as well as block it.

There are Encryptors available that work with land line phones and cells to ensure tapping and eavesdropping cannot happen. You will need one on both ends. Your voice is converted into scrambled analog signals. Anyone listening without the other Encryptor will not be able to understand a thing.

There are hardware and software that can intercept cell phone conversations. It is called a phone interceptor. If you are a parent you may want this because you can use GPS to know where your children are at, at all times.

You can call the phone and listen to the surroundings when it is not being used. Or you can call during a conversation and listen to both sides of the call. No ringing will be heard on the receiving end. You can also keep track of all incoming and outgoing test messages. Do you have a cheating spouse?

Sometime rumors are true. One rumor I am aware of is if you have an answering machine and it beeps your phone is tapped. I believe it from my personal experience. And the fact that I came across someone on the internet trying to say it just was not true. Question everyone who professes to be an authority.

I was entering a department store and observed a woman park in the back of the parking lot. I waited for her and told her that was not a wise place to park. She asked my why and I stated, "At the back of the parking lot no one could see her if she were to be attacked". She told me she had gotten this advice at a rape prevention meeting. I then asked if it was a male speaker. Here answer of yes did not surprise me and I then asked her what else he had said. He had told her to park next to a van if she saw one. I told her "Vans are the vehicle of choice of rapists".

Protecting our children from Predators

I am adding this material because I believe the general public chooses to deny that this can happen. As I stated previously I have a son with a handicap and spent a good deal of time in hospitals when he was younger. I remember watching one mother cry because her son had been molested by her boyfriend whom she trusted to watch him. He died from the loss of blood. Another 4-year-old girl came to the hospital running yet another unexplainable fever. Despite all the tests the doctors could not figure out what caused the fever. I can still remember her shaking her head yes when I asked if someone was putting something in her urinary tract. The first and singularly important thing to do when a child or someone tells you that they have been hurt is believe them. You will lose their trust and make the road to recovery so much more difficult.

Rape on college campuses is a huge problem nationally. Secretary of Education Arne Duncan, put it this way: "Every school would like to think it's immune from sexual violence but the facts suggest otherwise. According to one widely referenced study 1 in 5 women is sexually assaulted while in college."

Under the landmark Title IX legislation, Duncan said, schools have an obligation to ensure students impacted by this get justice and also the help they need to complete their education: "We know that if children and young people aren't safe they can't learn. It's as simple and as fundamental of a problem as that."

Most universities and colleges, however, fail to take adequate measures to prevent sexual assault on campus, the U.S. Department of Education said in a 2011 "Dear Colleague" letter. About 20% of women and 6% of men are victims of completed or attempted sexual assaults during college.

It has only been in the past decade or so that legislation has begun to address this crisis of rape on college campuses. Why? Schools did not want parents knowing they had a problem so they would send their little girls there. Some actively covered it up. Make it a point to ask how many sexual assaults they have had when considering a college to attend. It is no longer just a woman's problem. It is required by law now that regular reports are issued to the students about campus crimes. Also ask them what they have and will do for a victim. Be very leery of colleges that are big on sports.

If you are underage do not accept drinks. You are too easy to be intoxicated and taken advantage of. Only drink something that you have opened yourself. Alcohol is still the number one drug used to incapacitate victims. Never go to a party that you do not know anyone. Never go alone. Always have someone who will stick with you and protect you. Some date raped drugs if given too much of can be fatal. There are usually some telltale signs that a sexual assault has taken place. You may have swelling and soreness, bruising, and possibly abrasions of the genital and anal areas. You also may find bruising about your extremities where you may have been held down.

To combat growing child prostitution, federal agencies formed the Innocence Lost National Initiative in June 2003 to address enterprises involved in the domestic sex trafficking of children. Those agencies were the FBI's Criminal Investigative Division, the Department of Justice's Child Exploitation-Obscenity Section and the National Center for Missing and Exploited Children.

A three-day federal crackdown on child prostitution rings across the country has resulted in the recovery of 69 children and the arrest of 884 people, including 99 pimps, federal authorities said in November of 2010. Still want to let your children run free on the internet? American children are being sold for sex in this country not some other third world country.

There are now 39 Innocence Lost task forces and working groups throughout the country. The FBI says that at least 25 percent of adult prostitutes were enticed into the illegal activity as juveniles. So far, those units have recovered 1,250 children, and the initiative has resulted in 438 indictments, 625 convictions, 153 criminal enterprises disrupted and 58 successfully dismantled, authorities said. Convictions have resulted in sentences ranging up to 25-years-to-life and in the seizure of more than $3 million in assets, authorities said.

Statistics indicate that most female runaways will be forced out on the street as hookers within 72 hours. Some will be gang raped to lower their self-esteem so they can work the streets. Still want to run away? I recall a case from the news of a 15-year-old runaway that was captured by two 18-year-olds (male and female) and kept in a box under a bed. She only got out for sex. If you are being sexually abused at home running away is not the answer nor will it make you any safer. Report any abuse to the authorities. There are some cased where under aged boys and girls are kidnapped and forced into prostitution but most are seduced by men who make them feel loved and offer other securities. If you are a father make sure your child does not need love and security from another man.

Some young girls are recruited by other girls for their pimps. Always know who your daughter associates with. Sex trafficking does not discriminate and preys upon vulnerability. The average age a girl is when first being prostituted is 13. Be wary of older boyfriends. In short trafficker's prey on the most vulnerable of society. Once a girl enters the world of prostitution they have a 7-year life expectancy with homicide and aids as the main source of death. Then there is the fact that prostitutes commit suicide at a rate 45 times that of the general population.

One pimp let a girl go because she had reached her shelf life. Usually they kill them so there will not be a living witness against them. The drugs they will hook you on to keep you dependent on them take a toll.

Another raid dubbed Operation Dark Night captured 43 criminals and freed 11 sex slaves in Georgia, Florida, North and South Carolina. One woman was kept in a 10 X 12 box with a small bed where she performed sex acts. The detailed indictment details how some victims would sometimes service 30 or more men a day, all for 30 Dollars each. The road to recovery for these victims is a long one. The most deprived thing is that most if not all of the Johns had to know something was wrong but never reported it. Sadly, this is just the tip of the ice burg.

Traffickers use a variety of tactics -- both online and in person to trap their victims. Profits from human trafficking are estimated at $32 billion, $15.5 billion of which comes from industrialized nations, according to a 2005 report from the International Labor Organization. According to the FBI, an estimated 293,000 American youth are at risk

According to San Antonio Police Detective George Segura, gangs look for girls on Facebook who are showing off a bit too much skin, and are possibly seeking attention. Gang members then approach the girls on Facebook, befriend them, and convince them to meet up in person. No one is too young to be exploited — police say girls as young as 12 are being recruited. The sex trade is big business for gangs. According to a Bexar County probation officer, gang members "can easily make hundreds of thousands of dollars per girl, per year." Girls as young as 12 are being lured into prostitution. That age is too young to be on the internet particularly social sites like Facebook.

I was at a zoo with my son and there was a woman and her daughter there that was taking a lot of selfies with a tablet. I eventually asked why she took so many. She told me she had a Facebook friend who wanted to know where she was. When I found out she did not know who it was I told her she should delete them immediately; she was very likely being stalked. Even some older children are not safe on social sites.

According to www.Sex-Offenders.us: A child is molested every four seconds. Nearly one out of every three girls and one of every four boys is molested by age 18. This difference in these numbers may be because boys report molestation less frequently than girls.

Adults were the offender in 60% of the sexual assaults of youth under age 12. Rarely were the offenders of young victim's strangers. Strangers were the offender in just 3% of sexual assaults against victims under age 6 and 5% of the sexual assault of victimizations of youth ages 6 through 11.-Sexual Assault of Young Children as Reported to Law Enforcement, 7/00, NCJ 182990, U.S. Department of Justice

• 1 in 5 violent offenders serving time in a state prison reported having victimized a child.- BJS Survey of State Prison Inmates, 1991

• 2/3 of all prisoners convicted of rape or sexual assault had committed their crime against a child. - BJS Survey of State Prison Inmates, 1991

The most dangerous people are the ones you know and trust.

What, you cannot believe a human being can commit these actions against another human being and, especially, against innocent children? Why because you would not? I have seen very real pictures of young children beheaded so nothing should shock you as being unbelievable. Especially if a child tells you someone has done something to them; believe them.

Do you feel helpless in not knowing what to do to protect your child? There should be nothing you won't do to protect them.

* **Every 40 seconds**, in the United States alone, a child is reported missing or abducted.

* **1.5 million Children** are abducted each year. Can you imagine what this figure must be worldwide?

* With approximately 75 million children in the United States, every person has a 1% chance of being snatched away before surviving to adulthood to a parent (even 1% is 1% too much!)

* Of child kidnapping victims, **40% are killed, 4% are never found, with 71% being taken by a complete stranger**

* Most abductions occur within a quarter of a mile from the victim's home

* 32% of child abductions take place on a street or in a car, while another 25% of abductions take place in a park or a wooded area

* In 46% of child abductions **(almost half)**, the child is sexually assaulted

* More than **70% of kidnapping victims are girls**

* 75% of kidnapped children are murdered within three hours of their abduction

Taken from the U.S. Department of Justice Bureau of Justice Statistics.

Many child molesters know their victims. Some stalk their victims, observing their habits as they walk to and from school. They often try to buy houses near schools or parks.

Pedophiles have a strong, almost irresistible, desire to have sex with children. The average pedophile molests 260 victims during their lifetime. Over 90% of convicted pedophiles are arrested again for the same offense after their release from prison.

The best protection is to help your children learn to resist unwanted advances and to learn about threats in your neighborhood.

Visit www.Sex-Offenders.us for resisted offenders in your neighborhood or http://www.nsopw.gov/en. I found 20 listed for my zip code.

"There are 400,000 registered sex offenders in the United States, and an estimated 80,000 to 100,000 of them are missing. They're supposed to be registered, but we don't know where they are and we don't know where they're living". - Ernie Allen, President of the National Center for Missing Exploited Children to co-anchor Hannah Storm on *The Early Show*

A male victim of rape without intervention ends up becoming a predator himself. This does not excuse their behavior but more has to be done to encourage them to come forward to receive help. Historically, rape has been viewed as a crime against women. Only recently did the government change the law to include males. I believe more has to be done to protect them in the first place. I introduced a petition on Whitehouse.gov to make chemical castration mandatory for anyone who forcibly molests a minor. This is the only sure fired way to break the cycle of violence. I have had two women ask me if rape can be prevented. YES IT CAN! The system is failing miserably and this is a very effective and low-cost method that will do more to prevent rape than anything currently utilized.

When I was 12 my parents had a friend that did not seem right in the head to me. One day he showed up at our door and wanted me to play with him. Even at 12 it seemed odd for me to play with a married man that had kids. About a week or so later his wife showed up telling me it was a very good thing I had not. One predator told me that child molesters are just adults that have never grown up doing adult things with children. Then there was the one I knew that prayed on the church because he knew how to play on their weakness that they must forgive sinners.

I remember talking with a 3 or 4-year-old girl one time. Evidently her parents had been telling her about perverts that like little girls. She asked me what they did to little girls and I said, "they like to hurt them". She asked me how. I said I could not say but "it would probably hurt just like they but a nail right through your little arm". Feel free to use this yourself.

Would your kids go home with a stranger? You need to test them. 20 children were tested after being told not to talk to strangers or go with them. Despite that 7 of the 20 went with a stranger.

I am not going to propagate how they were lured away but just telling them is not enough. It is important to teach them that strangers look nice as well. They need to develop critical thinking.

Young today are more often than not left to their own devices to choose what is and is not right. This is especially true online. Teen boys are the largest consumers of online pornography. According to a 2007 Alberta study, 90 per cent of teen boys and 70 per cent of teen girls say they have viewed sexually explicit material on the Internet at least once. One third of the boys say they have watched porno films "too many times to count". Numerous concerns relating to young people's exposure to explicit sexual depictions have been raised by health professionals. These include becoming sexually active at earlier ages, experiencing increased violence or abuse in sexual relations, increased acceptance of sexual stereotypes and increased obsession with body image.

Set the computer in a living room or other busy area so kids are not on the internet unsupervised. I read an article about a key logger that looked like a charger. Kids that are internet savvy know how to delete their internet history. Kids will become curious about the opposite sex so you need to be able to talk to them because pornography is not a healthy alternative. Install pop-up blockers and search out software like Net Nanny.

I learnt of an incident where a woman gave a 12-year-old girl a pamphlet about how to become a prostitute. That was exactly what that little girl did. The woman went to jail. Young that are left to their own devices will chose wrong every time. Be in your child's life in everything they do that you can. Do not wait for them to tell you; ask them if anyone is touching them in inappropriate places. Always believe them and never call them liars. One rapist said he might not have become one if someone had believed him when he was assaulted.

The following material is added with permission of Protect Massachusetts Children

The Warning Signs of Abuse in Children

- Behavioral changes, extreme mood swings, withdrawal, fearfulness & excessive crying.
- Bed-wetting, nightmares, fear of going to bed or other sleep disturbances.
- Acting out with inappropriate sexual activity or showing an unusual interest in sexual matters.
- A sudden acting out of aggressive or rebellious behavior.
- School or behavioral problems.
- Changes in toilet-training habits.
- A fear of certain places, people or activities.
- Bruises, rashes, cuts, limping; multiple or poorly explained injuries.
- Sexual activities with toys or other children, such as simulating sex with dolls or asking other children / siblings to behave sexually.
- New words for private body parts.
- Cutting or burning herself or himself as an adolescent.
- Some children who are molested may not show any of these symptoms. Some child molesters groom their victims so successfully that the children love them and even try to protect them.

How Does it Happen?

- A predator will win your child's love and trust with treats, attention, and "love." If he or she is not getting love and attention from you, they will get it from someone else.
- Predators convince children they are responsible for their behavior.

- They make your child think no one will believe them if they tell.
- They tell your child you will be disappointed in them for what they have done "with" them.
- They warn your child they will be punished if they tell.
- They may threaten your child with physical violence against them, you, a pet, or other loved ones.
- They will shame your child into keeping the abuse secret.
- They may make the child feel sorry for them.
- They will do anything and say anything to keep assaulting your child and to keep your child from telling.
- Children usually keep sexual abuse a secret because of the shame and guilt they feel. They may also fear that no one will believe them if they talk about the abuse or they may have been threatened by their abuser not to tell.

A Child Predator:

- May work or volunteer at businesses that cater to children. Child predators commonly seek relationships with adults who have children in the home. Single parent families make particularly good targets.
- Can be of any race, have any religious belief, and have any sexual preference
- Could be a parent, step-parent, relative, friend, teacher, clergyman, baby-sitter, anyone.
- Is likely to be a stable, employed, respected member of the community.
- May "accidentally" expose himself / herself or walk in on children unexpectedly.
- May use situations like tucking kids in at night to touch them sexually.
- May have told your child "this is normal; it is what all fathers do.
- May be so good at manipulating children that your child may try to protect them.

- Can be a man, woman, married or single.
- Can be a child, adolescent, or adult.
- Is probably well liked by you and your child.

Massachusetts Statistics

- In 2003 Massachusetts had the third highest rate of child abuse among the 50 states, with 22 out of every 1,000 children being a victim. ~ *U.S. Department of Health and Human Services*
- In 2007 Massachusetts had the highest rate of confirmed cases of child abuse and neglect in the country. The rate was twice the national average. ~ *U.S Department of Health and Human Services*
- *In 2008 Massachusetts had the highest rate of confirmed cases of child abuse and neglect in the country. The rate was twice the national average. ~ U.S Department of Health and Human Services*
- In 2009 Massachusetts had the highest rate of confirmed cases of child abuse and neglect in the country. The rate was twice the national average. ~ *U.S Department of Health and Human Services*
- On average, 290 children were reported abused each day. ~ *Massachusetts Department of Social Services (2003)*
- On average, there are more than 30 sex offenders per city and town in Massachusetts.

National Statistics

- The average pedophile has 244 victims in their lifetime. ~ *National Institute of Mental Health*
- Children who have been sexually abused are 2.5 times more likely to develop alcohol abuse, while children who have been sexually abused are 3.80 times more likely to develop drug addictions. ~ *National Institute on drug abuse 2000 report*

- Only 1 to 2 percent of child sexual abusers are strangers to their victims. ~ *Prevention Child Abuse America*
- Sex offenders are 4.5 times more likely than other criminals to be re-arrested for sexual assault. ~ *Massachusetts Family Institute*
- Nearly 4 in 10 violent sex offenders serving time in state prisons reported that their victims were age 12 or younger. ~ *U.S. Department of Justice*

What do you do if your child is abused?

- If your child discloses abuse to you, remain calm, listen, and reassure them that the abuse is not their fault and that you are glad they told you.
- Call your local police department or child abuse hotline and report the abuse. By failing to notify the authorities you may unwittingly lead to the abuse of other children. ***Do not try to handle the situation yourself.*** It is crucial to your child that you report abuse and pursue prosecution.
- Taking the necessary steps to get the abuser off the streets provides children with a sense of security, as well as the opportunity to get justice.
- In order to avoid confusion, anxiety or guilt, children should never overhear conversations about their disclosure. Likewise, you should seek support and comfort for yourself where your child can't see or hear what you say.
- The prognosis for healing after being molested is better for children who are supported and believed when they disclose. Listen to your kids, and pay attention to their behavior.

The following info is from
http://www.protectkids.com/index.html which is written by
Donna Rice Hughes

Pornography's Relationship to Rape and Sexual Violence

According to one study, early exposure (under fourteen years of age) to pornography is related to greater involvement in deviant sexual practice, particularly rape. Slightly more than one-third of the child molesters and rapists in this study claimed to have at least occasionally been incited to commit an offense by exposure to pornography. Among the child molesters incited, the study reported that 53 percent of them deliberately used the stimuli of pornography as they prepared to offend. [i]

The habitual consumption of pornography can result in a diminished satisfaction with mild forms of pornography and a correspondingly strong desire for more deviant and violent material.

Pornography's Relationship to Child Molestation

In a study of convicted child molesters, 77 percent of those who molested boys and 87 percent of those who molested girls admitted to the habitual use of pornography in the commission of their crimes. Besides stimulating the perpetrator, pornography facilitates child molestation in several ways. For example, pedophiles use pornographic photos to demonstrate to their victims what they want them to do. They also use them to arouse a child or to lower a child's inhibitions and communicate to the unsuspecting child that a particular sexual activity is okay: "This person is enjoying it; so will you."

Exposure to Pornography May Incite Children to Act Out Sexually against Other Children.

Exposure to Pornography Shapes Attitudes and Values

Exposure to Pornography Interferes with a Child's Development and Identity

Even if you use preventative tools such as an Internet filter at home, remember to ask your children these questions, especially if they are using the Internet outside of your home.

> Have you seen any pornographic pictures?
> Has anyone online talked dirty to you?
> Have you met anyone online whom you don't know?
> Has anyone asked you for personal information?
> Has anyone asked to meet you in person?

What a Safe Harbour Law Does

Safe Harbour laws were developed by states to address inconsistencies with how children that are exploited for commercial sex are treated. Under federal law, a child under eighteen that is induced into providing commercial sex is a victim of trafficking and must be treated as such. State laws criminalize adults that have sex with children under statutory rape laws, however these laws were not applied in cases where the adult purchased sex. The result was children, recognized under both state and federal law as victims of a crime, were arrested and convicted of prostitution. Safe Harbour laws are intended to address the inconsistent treatment of children, raise awareness about children that have been commercially sexually exploited, and ensure that these victims were provided with services rather than a criminal conviction. From www.Polarisproject.org

To get help or report a tip call text 1888-373-7888 National Human Trafficking Hotline.

Reporting child abuse is the first step toward preventing it. Victims of child abuse often get into abusive relationships. Child abuse can mutate into a form of PTSD — and the signs of it can manifest into the victim's adulthood. This PTSD include aggressive behavior, night terrors, and loss of interest in everyday activities. When these children become adults, they disassociate themselves to cope with abuse at a young age. https://www.havoca.org/ is one resource for adult victims of child abuse.

Scanners

Predators have to have a method of listen to the electronic bugs that they have planted somehow. Most scanners operate in the public frequency range that the police and fire service use. The higher frequencies of some bugs will have to be divided into the lower ones used by the scanner to be picked up. A recorder can also be used that will activate only when there is a signal from the victim, eliminating the old stake out.

Having a background in electronics, I get catalogs in the mail now and then. Do business with a company and it is sure to send you one free. One that I received dealt with radios and the like with an educational section to make it appealing as a newsletter. One catalog had directions on how to take a specific scanner and alter it so a person could increase the frequency range so that those cordless phones could be listened in on. Books have been published on how to change scanners as well. These phones have a limited range of less than 1000 feet or so. There are a few pre-amplifiers available that attach to the scanner's antenna, which increases their reception range. For the most part, keep an eye out in your neighborhood for strangers.

I once knew a woman whose husband had left her for another woman. He wanted to keep the house, so he had hired a PI to watch her. When talking to me on her portable phone, she described her neighborhood as not having many houses around and that there were two men sitting in a car at the side of the road. Every time I made her laugh, she said they laughed too. Manufacturers may change the transmitted frequencies, but rest assured someone will find a way of listening in. Newt Gingrich used to be the house speaker until someone just driving around with a modified scanner listened in on him getting insider information about stocks.

This subject came up when my chiropractor was asking me what I thought about wireless internet connections. When I told him about this ability of scanners, he told me how just the other night his baby monitor was picking up both sides of his neighbor's phone conversation. His wife told him that that was enough of that when they started discussing how one of them used to sell drugs.

Security systems

It makes me cringe when I hear someone refer to an alarm system as a security system. Just what security does it provide? None, it will do nothing to protect you. It is just what its name says; it's an alarm. Granted that will be a help, but it will not stop someone from doing anything to you. For that, you need something that will provide you with protection and security. Bars on the window, a dog, a panic room or something from Smith and Wesson are the only things that provide real security.

Yes, there are areas where crime is so bad that people put bars on their windows. Not somewhere I would want to live but it works. They also have been known to keep people in, in the event of a fire. A panic room is something I recommend. Dogs, however, are not always reliable and may turn on you or a child. Select a proper breed and train them so they will not bark at just anything; only then will they prove to be a good alarm. The purchase of a shock collar is the best way to accomplish this. If you don't like cleaning up after them, I recommend the electrical kind.

If you are going to use motion detectors, you will have to have an area to keep your dog away because they will be able to hear the high frequency these sensors emit. Faced with getting a dog or a motion sensor etc. I would pick the sensor. Dogs are so unreliable. You must feed them and take them to the vet. Both of which are far more expensive than a motion detector.

Now back to the Smith and Wesson. They manufacture guns for those of you who did not know that. Guns can be a good deterrent without even being fired. However, if you pick one up, you had better be prepared to use one if needed. Your attacker could take it away from you and use it on you or someone else later. I was sitting in a ground floor room late one night with two women. The room had a sliding glass door with a full-length curtain. Then one of the women in a terrified voice screams, "My God someone is trying to get in the room!" To which I walked over to the window, pulled back the curtain with my left hand and, sure enough, there was someone out there in a white tee shirt. It was quite dark so that was about all I could make out. One look at the gun in my right hand inspired the would-be intruder to run.

Hiding security cameras or, if you prefer, finding them

Cameras that are wired to a monitor and/or recorder will not radiate any electronic signal that can be detected with a bug detector. Now video bugs are being made so a predator can literally be the fly on the wall. Cameras have been hidden for a while now. I found one disguised as a screw. I found one that transmits audio and video at 2.4 Gig herz in color for 0.6 miles. One was made to look like a cell phone that could record for 16 hours.

Pinhole cameras are very small but must protrude into the target room to work. White out will help them to blend into the wall. If you are placing one in your home, use the same paint that you used on the walls. Look for these above eye level. When was the last time you looked up at the ceiling? People just do not look up.

I once had a job interview where they gave me a two-hour written test and put me in a room with one other guy. While walking out after the test, they informed me that the other guy had looked at my test while I went to the bathroom. Then they became embarrassed when they realized they had given away the secret that the only way for them to know this was that they had covert cameras in the room.

I was also given a written test in another job interview and was left in a room by myself but this time one blind was left open. Well; being alone I took the opportunity to pull out the cheat sheet I had brought along just in case the opportunity presented itself. It was a rather small company, so when the phone rang, I could hear it. I also heard everyone shout (cheer) at the same time. I took one look at the open blind and wondered if they knew I was using a cheat sheet. Well, months later when I finally got the job, the supervisor told me they had hired a private detective to watch me.

Two-way mirrors of course will conceal cameras or people. The adage you get what you pay for applies to two-way mirrors. Some mirrors you can just look at and tell they are two-way. For the really good ones hold a pencil up to it. Do this on your medicine cabinet and you will see that the tips do not touch. If they do then it is a two-way mirror. Shining a really bright light at one will also prove revealing. Next time you are in a gas station restroom you might want to try this.

Speaker screens are not opaque and can be used to hide a camera and will work quite well. There are many things that can hide a camera today. Exit signs, tissue boxes, lights, fake cell phones, even pens. They even come in teddy bears.

Do a search on E-bay or the internet for "Bug Detector Hidden Camera Laser Lens". I seriously doubt this is a true laser but it will make a hidden camera reflect its light and show up through the filter even when the camera is off. I set a small camera on my TV and it showed up from across the room and it was not on. It was real cheap and would fit in a woman's purse real easy. I don't have much faith in its RF detection abilities. It did pick up my cordless phone when it was on.

This means buy something else to find electronic bugs. Sometimes public bathrooms are not so private and a small camera detector might be a good thing to have.

Sometime hidden cameras are a good thing. Sorry for not having dates and fact but a 12-year-old girl disappeared in Florida and was found dead some time later. She had been kidnapped while walking through a car wash which was caught on camera and her murderer was caught. Melanie and Byrd Billings, known for adopting a large brood of children with special needs, were shot to death in their home in Pensacola Florida during a robbery. An extensive security system captured the whole thing leading to arrests.

Apparently, the person assigned to turning it off did not. Which means they knew about it. They had rehearsed for 30 days. Having a security system is good. Having a hidden back up recorder is even better.

I keep hearing of incidences where more hidden cameras are being detected that were used to spy on women. The most recent one was a female officer aboard a US submarine. Do not simply dismiss this, arm yourself to ensure your privacy is yours alone. Rest assured those being detected is just the tip of the iceberg as they say.

Image enhancers can be used to improve poor quality video from security cameras meaning even a poor-quality video recorder is better than none. I still remember a poor-quality video that was played on television of a home invasion and murder.

Seeing in the Dark

First let's discuss some facts about the human eye. Most of us certainly know that the pupil is the opening in the center of the eye that opens and closes to regulate the amount of light that can enter. We all know that it takes some time for the pupil to react when going from a very light to a very dark situation and vice versa. When going from a bright spot to a dark one, it is possible to speed up this adjustment time by closing one's eyes just prior to entering the dark room. This works because by closing your eyes, you are depriving them of light and the pupils will compensate for this loss by opening more, thus being adjusted when you reopen them in the dark room. Try it, this works when you practice the timing right. When walking from a bright room into a dark one, close your eyes about 10 feet before the door while still walking. If you are real clumsy, be prepared to run into things, so walk slowly. Sorry, but this will not work when going from a very dark room to a bright one. You will just have to suck it up.

Our retina is covered with rods and cones. We use the rods for black and white at night in low-light situations. The area where the optic disk leaves the retina causes a blind spot in our vision, most apparent in our rods. This blind spot is about in the center of our vision. If you need to get somewhere in a hurry in the dark, concentrate on focusing your vision at a 45-degree angle to where you want to go. This will move the blind spot away from the direction you want to go in. If you are either fleeing from or pursuing someone in the woods, you had better have a better concentration span than I do. The more moonlight there is, the better this will work. If you lose your focus for an instant you could very well run into a tree. Just do not run at full tilt because you could just knock yourself out.

Speaking of trees, they all look alike in the dark. You can be in an area you know like the back of your hand but at night you will not recognize a thing. So, if you ever get lost in the woods, even if you're in a familiar area, stay put until sunrise.

Unless of course it is going to go to -10 degrees then get yourself out of the woods at all cost. If you are lost in the winter and its snowy or the ground is frozen, and if you need to sleep, find a Christmas tree and cut the limbs off and make a bed with them. These will keep you off the ground which will draw all your heat from you if you lie down on it.

So, you ask, what does this have to do with how safe I am? Well, this information will help you when in a fight or flight situation.

SEXUAL ASSAULT

The sad facts are that there are rapists out there, lying in wait. A best guess is there is a forcible rape every six minutes in America. A newspaper article in the early '80s calculated that by the year 2000, one out of every three women would have been raped *at least* once. Unfortunately, gang rape has also been on the rise. From a newspaper article that I clipped from a paper in 1985, between 1973 and 1982 an estimated 1.5 million women and an estimated 123,000 males were victims of rape.

Most psychologists agree that rape is not for sexual desire but the result of anger or the need to assert power. The majority of rapists are young men who have sexual outlets available to them. They are either married to or dating women with whom they voluntarily have sex.

When anger against women is the motive, the perpetrators are violent and unpremeditated with the intent to degrade their victim. Beware of drug users, as some drugs induce great fits of rage, as does alcohol in some people. I remember reading an article about a man who dragged a woman around behind a building at a party and shot her in the head. One time that my son was in the hospital a three-year-old boy was admitted whose mother had beaten him over forty percent of his body in a drug-induced rage. I can still remember his crying. Before he left, he was displaying violence against the nurses. Violence against women cannot be justified, but I am sure this played out throughout his life. Hitler's hatred of the Jews was traced back to one woman.

Rapes that are motivated by the need to assert power are pre-planned and the victim is stalked. This type of rapist may be compensating for feelings of helplessness. This type will also display a need to control people in other ways as well.

Never date the schoolyard bully or the grown ones. He likes to control people, and that is what rape is about, the ultimate control over someone else. Psychologists can attest to the fact that this desire to control spills over into other aspects of rapists' lives. Which is why DNA testing is now the law whenever an arrest is made. Avoid arrogant people. To see a pretty woman and just take her, if that is not arrogant, what is?

Even if all you can do is drop a dime to call the police, you should still do so. Definitely do not stand around and do nothing or idolize the rapist as some sort of a hero. If you are the victim and you get any help from somebody make it a point to say thank you. I can only remember 3 times someone has thanked me.

With the rise in the number of homosexuals, rape is no longer a problem just for women only. Women also attack other woman. In January of 2012 the Justice Department changed the definition of rape to now include men. The crime of rape will be defined as "penetration, no matter how slight, of the vagina or anus with any body part or object, or oral penetration by a sex organ of another person, without the consent of the victim," a Justice Department statement said. Let's not forget about child molesters either. This means that no matter who you are, there is a chance that it could happen to you.

The revised definition includes any gender of victim or perpetrator. It also includes instances in which a victim is incapable of giving consent because of mental or physical incapacity, such as intoxication. Physical resistance is not required to demonstrate lack of consent. In 2010, the FBI reported a forcible rape every 6.2 seconds. With a broader definition, that statistic will probably be even more horrific, said Mai Fernandez, executive director of the National Center for Victims of Crime.

It would be a good idea to discuss this subject with your spouse or potential mate, since many marriages do not survive sexual assault. I will give you a hint, guys: it does not help to accuse women of 'asking for it' to protect your male egos. It would help for you to tell them that you love them, and that no man can ever steal that away from them.

Consider two women for a moment: one is a woman who, having no conscience commits adultery and hides it from her husband; the other is a woman who has been raped, but also hides it from her husband and faces him every day as if nothing had happened. There is no difference between the two, for the husband's marriage bed has been defiled. In both cases, the woman is hiding something from her husband. The bottom line here is that a real lady could not face her husband every day and hide something like rape from him. This should be discussed before marriage by all couples.

Rape is not a crime of passion, but one of physical violence and domination motivated by sexual gratification. It is the ultimate control over another person. So, never date the schoolyard bully. I am not going to delve into the different types of forced raped, but if you think being beaten is passionate, you should seek psychological counseling.

Although some people may tell you that being raped is simply like having sex with someone whom you did not want to have it with, this assertion is wrong. As stated before, it is not just sex. If it were, then perhaps they should legalize rape. After all, if it is just sex, so what if they have to hold you down? Some people accuse me of making too much of it. It can and does render some women insane some temporary some permanent. It does not sound like a small thing when one rape victim counsels a new victim and tells her there will come a time when she will be able to forget it for a whole day.

After you have been raped, there will never be a day in the rest of your life when you will not be a victim.

Initially a victim is in shock and often will ask in disbelief "Why me?" After the initial fear and anxiety, other symptoms will manifest themselves. They may lose their appetites, develop headaches (resulting from the silent rage that rape is often called), insomnia and fatigue. Some will be plagued by nightmares and irrational fears for years afterwards. Some will become unable to maintain a job as well as maintain a normal sex life. These symptoms may persist for years afterwards.

This is one instance where an ounce of prevention is worth more than a pound of cure. Sexual assault can and does happen anywhere, anytime. I know of an instance where a bank teller was raped at her bank during business hours. And no one stopped it. Given the number of sexually transmitted diseases today and the frequency of rape, I would suggest getting any vaccines that are or become available to prevent contracting one.

I heard from a nurse of a two-year-old girl that was molested and got genital warts from it. A rapist clearly has little consideration or thought for his victim, so sharing a disease is not going to bother him either. Know that there is never a time when someone with genital warts is not contagious, vaccination is a good idea if you are very sexually active, especially if strangers are your cup of tea.

It is certainly not my desire to educate the public on ways to commit this heinous crime. I also recommend that you look carefully at any and all advice you are given to avoid rape. Yes, even mine, for I am hardly an expert either. Incidentally, a woman juror is 35% harder to convince of rape than a man is.

There are many statistics about rape. The ones I am about to share are gleaned from my memory of what has been disseminated through the media.

40% of all rapes started out as a simple burglary.

40% of all rapes happen in the daytime.

80% of victims know their attackers.

The average rapist has 25-30 victims.

Most likely to be attacked are single women between the ages of 15-25.

12-34 are the highest risk years.

2.78 million Men in the U.S. have been victims of sexual assault or rape.

Pornography encourages rape by depersonalizing women.

According to the U.S. Department of Justice, 1 in 4 rapes take place in the victim's home. Two in 10 rapes take place at the home of a friend, neighbor or relative. And almost two-thirds of all rapes are committed by someone the victim already knows. Experts say there are two things a rapist looks for when he tracks a victim: opportunity and vulnerability. That somehow, provocative clothing invites predatory behavior is a fabrication. "We, as a culture, like to blame the victim because it makes us feel safe," says Liz Roberts, the deputy CEO and chief program officer at Safe Horizon, a rape crisis center in New York City.

All, women included, have a subconscious belief that if women just did all the right things, like dressing modestly, then we would never be raped.

Here is some advice on how to prevent rape. Again, I am no expert, so examine my advice carefully. Even the so-called experts get it wrong. One University's instructions suggested vomiting and or urinating to prevent rape. You will likely do that all on your own without even trying to.

Never hitchhike or pick up a hitchhiker. Remember that I said it is not just a woman's problem any longer. Never live alone if you can help it. Do not publish your phone number; it will also list your address. Do not think using your first initial will fool anyone. Do not leave your car windows down when you park anywhere. Buy a car with air conditioning. Remote controls work in the summer also. Always lock the doors to your home and car. Do not ever tell a stranger where you live. Do not ever leave anything with your address on it in a public place (like trash cans). This applies to females of all ages. Do not ever tell anyone you could never go through a rape trial. Not even another woman; for I know of women who have helped their husbands commit rape. It is rare, but it can and does happen.

If you use an answering machine, get a male friend to record your message. Own a cell phone and carry it with you. Always know where you are. Again; never date a bully. He likes to control people, and that is what rape is about, the ultimate control over someone else. Avoid arrogant people. To see a pretty woman and just take her-- if that is not arrogant, what is? Neither men nor women should ever use or participate in pornography of any kind. It turns women into a piece of celluloid with no feelings or emotions.

Never have sex voluntarily with strangers. This will only serve to put credence to the myth that it is just sex and will do nothing to reinforce the respect men should have for women.

115

If you want men to have a higher level of respect for women, do not propagate the myth that it is just sex. Then once again men may be more willing to protect women. Make it harder to rape you than somebody else, this may sound cruel, yes, but the truth is rapists are out there. If you are ever raped, do not be ashamed of it, you are not alone. It happens to many women and men.

Carry mace and a cell phone. Start by following this advice, and then search for more. If you are raped, go to a hospital emergency room even if you are absolutely sure you could never prosecute. Doing so does not constitute pressing charges. Do not bathe shower or douche. Every hospital by law has someone trained to treat a rape victim. Do not let anyone touch you but that person. You could contract a sexually transmitted disease such as AIDS. They have an AZT cocktail to help you if your attacker does have AIDS. Yes, I know someone who was attacked by an individual with AIDS. While I was once in New Jersey, there were a couple of articles in the paper about just that type of attack.

Also, if you change your mind about pressing criminal charges later, it will be that much easier for you if you have gone to the hospital right away. DNA evidence that was collected makes it more than your word against his. You cannot simply plunk your butt down in the witness chair and say, I was raped. You will need all the proof you can get as well as being graphic. Then, if one or more of the jurors throw up, you have accurately described what it is like to be raped.

Lastly there is what is called repression (the burying of a painful feeling or thought from one's awareness) and false memories. An immediate record of the attack will hold much more water later on should you come forward. Especially if your attacker is a high-profile figure like say a popular comedian. I would say it bothered his victims a lot if they came forward years later.

There is no need to be ashamed if you have an orgasm during the rape. As I explained to a little girl whose father had raped her, if someone hits you it hurts because that is the way God made your body to work. Sex is the same way. It is just the way God made your body to work. Yes, it is horrible to be forced to have sex, but it does not mean you helped your attacker or asked for it. Nor that you helped them or deserved to be raped.

It is up to women to unite and prove that this will not be tolerated. It will not get any better until you send a message that you will no longer suffer quietly. In other words, more victims have to let rapists know that they have raped the wrong women.

Many women have asked how this could happen to them. Perhaps that is because society as a whole today still believes it only happens to women who deserve it. Realize that no one deserves to be raped, and everyone needs to stop viewing the victim as dirty. This includes other women as well. Only then will more women find the courage to come forward. The more that do come forward, the more rapists that will go to jail and the safer the world will be for all.

The bottom line is that anyone who makes the victim sorry is helping the rapist. Even the victim is helping the rapist if she does not come forward. Surprised? Remember that the average rapist has 25 victims, and if you do not report him, you are helping him to hurt someone else. I know that this will hurt many women, for this will be foremost on their minds. It is best to confront your demons right off. They will only get bigger later on. Certainly, some women do not report rape because of their lack of confidence in the legal system. You can't complain and say they failed you if you do not give the law a chance.

Incidentally, if you feel you are being persecuted or denied justice, call the FBI. Obstructing the law or harboring a fugitive from justice is illegal for everyone, and the FBI has a special division just for handling corrupt law enforcement officers,

117

even judges. You will find it listed in the front of your phone book, or call information. It has offices in Boston, Massachusetts and Roanoke, Virginia, to name just a few.

Rape can happen just about anywhere at any time; sometimes though it happens where the victim did not need to be. I am not trying to blame the victim; rape should never happen but it does. If you absolutely do not need to be there, then do not be there, especially at night. I recall an article that was in the paper some years ago about a woman who had disappeared from a bar and had left her coat and purse behind. This was a married woman with two children and she did not go there with her husband. When she did not come home by the next day, her husband reported her missing. Four months later, a woman's body was found at the bottom of a lake. Before positive identification was made, the paper reported that it could have been one of seven women that had gone missing in that time frame.

When you get right down to it, this whole book is about preventing rape. Anyone can write a book about that, but I write because I have more to share than most. Have no doubt that all the technology I have discussed can and is being used for that end. Remember sexual assault is a control thing and stalking is a part of that.

In the late-1980s there used to be a crippled man who sat in a wheelchair on Main St Worcester Mass. He kept a pail on a pool stick, which he used to collect donations for charities. He displayed a sign showing the amounts donated to each one. At one point, he was attacked by a man with a machete. He managed to survive the attack but died a few months later. With the economy being what it is, there are more panhandlers than ever before.

After a while, you recognize the regulars and the transients. There was one that I would see in an electric wheelchair. One

118

day coming home, I saw just the wheelchair. I ran into a group of police and told them about it. One of them replied that they were familiar with him and he was probably up walking around. He said I did not need to report anything. I told him about the machete attack and he could not believe anyone would do that. One of the other officers remembered it too, and I told him just because you would not do something like that does not mean someone else would not either. And that was a police officer; don't think for one minute that there are not rapists out there and that there is not a thing they would not do to rape. I know of one case where a woman lured other women to a location where her husband and friends would rape them. I was in court one day and I got to talking about rape with someone and a woman standing next to us could not believe that there could be a rapist in a courthouse. –Denial will not make you any safer perhaps place you at far more risk.

When in the Air Force, I was stationed in Virginia. Unfortunately, I spent all my money going home. Being young and passionate, I noticed a rather pretty woman. She had a boyfriend of another race who always had a friend with him. I saw them together quite often. I got to asking questions about them. It turns out that neither of them worked and had been in town for 3 months. Being a small town, gossip travels rapidly and had gotten back to them that I had been asking about them. I don't remember how, but all three of us ended up at the police station. So, I asked them where they were from, which they would not say. I asked them if they had a job and they stated they were on vacation. I asked them how they could afford to be on vacation for 3 months and they said something to the effect that friends were sending them money.

After they left, I encouraged the chief to follow the money. Since they were getting it through Western Union, it was a mere matter of finding out where it came from, which turned out to be New York, New York. The police there watched them and after identifying their prostitutes, picked them all up. It turns out

119

that each of the prostitutes had been romanced by one or the other of them and they were conned into moving away with them. Only, after arriving in NY they were gang raped and put out to work the streets.

Don't know if it was ever proven but there was the possibility that they had murdered one girl. I am a firm believer of learning from other people's mistakes, because you will never live long enough to make them all yourself.

You need to learn to keep your head and control your sympathetic nervous system. It controls the body's reactions to emergency situations. Intense fear or anger are results of action of this system. This is what make you faint ladies. I maintain that learning to control this is the most important thing you will learn from any defense classes.

Congress passed a disclosure law, now known as the Jeanne Clery Act that forces schools to disclose all crime that happens on campus so that students and their parents could be informed. The hope was to pressure college presidents to work on crime prevention. Instead, there have been many news stories of college campus cover ups. The more things change the more they stay the same. When choosing your college for your daughter make it a point to ask "Have you had any rapes?" Private colleges are just a business and have a vested interest in your children's enrolment. Originally known as the Campus Security Act, the *Jeanne Clery Disclosure of Campus Security Policy and Campus Crime Statistics Act* **(20 USC § 1092(f))** is the landmark federal law that requires colleges and universities across the United States to disclose information about crime on and around their campuses. The law is tied to an institution's participation in federal student financial aid programs and it applies to most institutions of higher education both public and private. The Clery Act is enforced by the United States Department of Education.

This was found on the internet and since the government cannot copyright anything I am including it. I am not trying to make myself an absolute authority on preventing rape and encourage you to never stop looking for information.

*"A friend of mine works in law enforcement and this email is being passed around to all the police officers and staff in her unit. The info in the email is not new information, but **rape crimes** have started to rise again, so it's being circulated again as a reminder. It contains some helpful **rape prevention tips**. Please pass this along and share it with your children and or friends."*

A group of rapists and date rapists in prison were interviewed on what they look for in a potential victim and here are some interesting facts:

My additions from here on are in italics and yes, I know I may be repeating myself.

1. The first thing men look for in a potential victim is hairstyle. They are most likely to go after a woman with a ponytail, bun, braid or other hairstyle that can easily be grabbed. They are also likely to go after a woman with long hair. Women with short hair are not common targets.

2. The second thing men look for is clothing. They will look for women whose clothing is easy to remove quickly. Many of them carry scissors around specifically to cut clothing.

3. They also look for women on their cell phone, searching through their purse, or doing other activities while walking because they are off-guard and can be easily overpowered.

4. Men are most likely to attack & rape in the early morning, between 5:00a.m. and 8:30a.m.

5. The number one place women are abducted from/attacked is grocery store parking lots. Number two is office parking lots/garages. Number three is public restrooms. *I've always wondered why it takes two women to go to the bathroom.*

Don't forget that rape can happen anywhere at any time but vehicles are a target of choice.

6. The thing about these men is that they are looking to grab a woman and quickly move her to another location where they don't have to worry about getting caught.

7. Only 2% said they carried weapons because rape carries a 3-5-year sentence but rape with a weapon is 15-20 years.

8. If you put up any kind of a fight at all, they get discouraged because it only takes a minute or two for them to realize that going after you isn't worth it because it will be time-consuming.

9. These men said they would not pick on women who have umbrellas, or other similar objects that can be used from a distance, in their hands. Keys are not a deterrent because you have to get really close to the attacker to use them as a weapon. So, the idea is to convince these guys you're not worth it.

10. If someone is coming toward you, hold out your hands in front of you and yell STOP or STAY BACK! Most of the rapists that were interviewed said they'd leave a woman alone if she yelled or showed that she would not be afraid to fight back. Remember, they are looking for an EASY target.

An easy target is also someone they think they can rape and get away with it. Always dress and carry yourself like a confident woman who cares about herself and is not likely to let anyone get away with raping her. Some rapists are opportunists and will rape only when they think they can get away with it. I was taking an evening college class where we had a few high school students with us. One evening in the lab there was just me the female instructor and a high school girl. The high school girl said to the instructor that she could never go through a rape trial. I told her "Never let those words out of your mouth ever again for the rest of your life." She asked why. I told her" That she was in no danger from me but she had just stood in front of a man and said" "Rape me I will never do anything about it" Then I told her that I know of cases where women helped their husbands rape women. Just because I do not discuss specific case does not mean I have no experience catching rapists. I am trying to educate you not impress.

The following tips have been learned through firsthand experience by fellow officers, witness and crime victim testimony, or from self-defense classes at the police academy.

1. If someone is following behind you on a street or in a garage or with you in an elevator or stairwell, look them in the face and ask them a question, like what time is it, or make general small talk: 'I can't believe it is so cold out here,' 'we're in for a bad winter.' Now you've seen their face and could identify them in a line-up; you lose appeal as a target.

This reminds me of a case I read about where a woman's attacker was brazen enough to walk right up to her on the sidewalk and say "Hello" then walk off. During the rape he just laughed when she told him her husband would be home soon. He knew enough about her to know she was not married. Never mind small talk go right to the real thing on your mind ask them "Are you following me?" Then do what #2 tells you to.

2. If you carry pepper spray (our instructor is a huge advocate of it and carries it with him wherever he goes), yell loudly I HAVE PEPPER SPRAY. Hold it out in plain sight and it will be a deterrent.

3. If someone grabs you, you can't beat them with strength but you can by outsmarting them. If you are grabbed around the waist from behind, pinch the attacker either under the arm (between the elbow and armpit) OR in the upper inner thigh VERY VERY HARD. One woman in our self-defense class said she used the underarm pinch on a guy who was trying to date rape her and was so upset she broke through the skin and tore out muscle strands - the guy needed stitches. Try pinching yourself in those places as hard as you can stand it - it hurts.

As I have said elsewhere when on a date provide your own transportation. I remember a young female doctor who attended my church and one day I saw her in a pickup truck with a guy.

I talked to her about it and she said it was a date. Then she told me how he wanted something after the date and complained how women always wanted him to spend money on them with nothing in return. I told her he was not a gentleman and if she continued to date him she could very well regret it. She did not go out with him again.

Two weeks later I showed her the newspaper he had gotten his name in for being arrested for date rape. I can still remember her fainting afterwards. I forgot about her sympathetic nervous system.

4. After the initial hit, always go for the GROIN. If you slap a guy's parts it is extremely painful. You might think that you'll anger the guy and make him want to hurt you more, but the thing these rapists told our instructor is that they want a woman who will not cause a lot of trouble. Start causing trouble and he's out of there.

5. When the guy puts his hands up to you, grab his first two fingers and bend them back as far as possible with as much pressure pushing down on them as possible.

My self-defense instructor did it to me without using much pressure, and I ended up on my knees and both knuckles cracked audibly.

If you fail this and you are grabbed say by both hands from the front do not try to strong arm your attacker. Reach up and grab him by his little fingers and pry them out to the point where you break them. This will not only bring him to his knees but he will have to seek medical attention which could lead to his arrest.

6. Of course, the things we always hear still apply. Always be aware of your surroundings, take someone with you if you can and if you see any odd behavior, don't dismiss it, go with your instincts! *Again, I say always carry a cell phone and know where you are if you need to summon help.*

7. If it is dark and/or you are unfamiliar with your surroundings, don't get into your car and then fasten your seatbelt. Start your car and drive away, fastening your seatbelt as you drive or at the next convenient stop. *Most purses have room for a flash light or get a little one that attaches to your key ring. Krypton bulbs are very bright. Some purses are made with an easily accessible center compartment meant to conceal a gun. Which I recommend but it can also make a flash light or mace just as easily accessible.*

8. If someone tries to get into your car or approaches your car in an aggressive manner, do not steer away from him. Instead, steer your car toward him; his automatic instinct will be to jump AWAY from the car. You may feel a little silly at the time, but you'd feel much worse if the guy really was trouble. *Your vehicle is a weapon don't be afraid to use it. Learn how.*

9. Tip from Tae Kwon Do - the elbow is the strongest point on your body. If you are close enough to use it, then do it!

10. One of our officers learned this from a tourist guide in New Orleans. If a robber asks for your wallet and/or purse, do NOT hand it to him. Toss it away from you ... chances are that he is more interested in your wallet and/or purse than in you, and he will go for the wallet/purse. So toss it and run like mad in the other direction! *This may work when you are a tourist but when you are on your home turf remember that your license with your address is in there.*

11. If you are ever thrown into the trunk of a car, kick out the back-tail lights and stick your arm out the hole and start waving like crazy. The driver won't see you, but everybody else will. This has saved lives.

12. Women have a tendency to get into their cars after shopping, eating, working, etc., and just sit (doing their checkbook, or making a list, etc.). DON'T DO THIS! The predator will be watching you, and this is the perfect opportunity for him to get in on the passenger side, put a gun to your head, and tell you where to go. As soon as you get into your car, lock the doors and leave.

13. If you do happen to get in your car and a stranger is inside and puts a gun to your head, DO NOT DRIVE OFF! Instead, gun the car engine and speed into anything, wrecking the car. Your air bag will save you. If the person is in the back seat, they will get the worst of it. As soon as the car crashes bail out and run. It is better than having them find your body in a remote location.

Carry a flash light and look inside your car before you get in. Also, if you open your door and the inside light does not come on run fast and hard. The chances of it being burnt out is far less likely than it was broken.

Always leave your car doors locked. Won't stop everyone but will make it harder to rape you. Ramming your car may sound

126

good in theory but it counts on your attacker being incapacitated in the crash. If not then all you have done is wreak your car. There is also no guarantee you will not be the one incapacitated. Another idea would be to install a kill switch and alarm that would go off when activated.

14. A few notes about getting into your car in a parking lot or parking garage:

a. Be aware at all times and look around you; look inside your car before entering it - look at the passenger side floor and in the back seat. *Always carry a small flashlight for this purpose.*

b. If you are parked next to a big van, enter your car from the passenger door. Most serial killers attack their victims by pulling them into their vans while the women are attempting to get into their cars.

c. Look at the car parked on the driver's side of your vehicle, and the passenger side. If a male is sitting alone in the seat nearest your car, you may want to walk back into the mall, or work, and get a guard/policeman to walk you back out.

15. It is always better to be safe than sorry - and better paranoid than dead.

16. Always take the elevator instead of the stairs. Stairwells are horrible places to be alone and the perfect crime spot. This is especially true at night.

I say never take an elevator. They stop at any floor and you never know who will enter. You don't have very much room to run either.

17. If the predator has a gun and you are not under his control, ALWAYS RUN! The predator will only hit you (a running target) 4 in 100 times. And even then, it most likely will not be a vital organ. RUN, preferably in a zig-zag pattern!

18. The majority of women usually try to be sympathetic without considering the potential danger. STOP doing this because it may get you raped or killed. Ted Bundy, the serial killer, was a good-looking, well-educated man, who ALWAYS played on the sympathies of unsuspecting women. He walked with a cane, or a limp, and often asked 'for help' into his vehicle or with his vehicle, which is when he abducted his next victim. *One guy would ask women to give him a ride home from a bar. Never be afraid to say no nor be rude if you have to when they persist.*

Please pass these rape prevention tips along to your friends and loved ones. It never hurts to be prepared in case of a criminal attack. If you have any other helpful info, feel free to share it by leaving a comment.

Street Smarts or All I Learned from the School of Hard Knocks

Well, not everything I learned. I read a book once that told me to learn from other people's mistakes. Worked pretty well for me in basic training, I never got written up once. Of course, it helps to be a really good runner when one must exit a female barracks in a hurry.

This material is about our world and not all of it is pretty. Therefore, we need to be able to recognize the importance of learning from other people's mistakes.

I once worked with a guy named Lenny. Now Lenny was a big guy. One day he came in from lunch and told us how he had found a needle on the ground by his car that was not there in the morning. Then he proceeded to show us where he had pricked his finger on it while picking it up. I told him he should go to the hospital, but he refused to. Remember he was a big guy, too big for me to handle if I had hit him on the head and knocked him out. I told him to at least tell his wife about it and to use a condom from then on. So, Lenny went on about his life as usual. A couple of years later after leaving that job, I run into another co-worker and we start to talk. He tells me that Lenny has AIDS and does not know how he got it and that his wife is about to leave him. I remind this co-worker about the needle with which Lenny pricked himself.

I have since then found one in a public park. Sad but true, there are people who are careless with needles and obviously do not care what they do with them. If you ever find a needle, DO NOT PICK IT UP. Call the police to have them dispose of it.

My son was born with a birth defect, so I have spent a lot of time in the hospital with him, some of that in ICU. One of the other patients once was an eight-year-old girl that had been found unconscious by her parents on the sidewalk in front of a store. This little girl almost died. It was two weeks before she could go home. I remember holding her and asking her how much she could remember before coming to the hospital. She could not remember anything about the week before she was found unconscious. It was some time later before she could remember drinking some blue liquid from a small vial that some man had given her. Why share this, you ask? Street smart your kids! It is sad but their innocent world is not so innocent any more. I was also in the emergency room when a rape victim came in. It is not a pretty sight ladies.

As I once explained to a child, it is not that every stranger is bad; it is just that you do not know you can trust them. Tell them to leave it up to the adults to decide who can be trusted. Explain that there are bad people out there; not everyone is bad, but until you know you can trust them, do not. It is important to educate children today, but do not create such paranoia that a child will live in fear. This could lead to an adult with some serious problems.

At the age of twelve, I lived in Jacksonville Florida. One day an old lady and her grand-daughter came down the street in a cart pulled by a seedy old horse. You remember the kind, with various bits of junk hanging off it. OK, I am old but not that old; this was not an everyday thing. Well anyways, this old lady gave me a candy bar, a Hershey's Almond Joy. Yes, my memory is that good. I could go on but I won't. Anyways, I showed it to my mother and upon inspection that candy bar had a little hole in the top. Needless to say, the next time that cart came around there were words exchanged. That was a long time ago.

The need to teach your children not to take anything from strangers, and if they do to show it to you, has only gotten worse. When I was 12 out trick or treating I went to a house that gave me a "special" apple.

Getting into cars with strangers is also a danger you need to teach your children not to do. My parents sent me to the store one time when I was ten. It was raining and I can still to this day remember some guy in a white car pulling up and telling me to get in. Not asking me, but telling me. I took off, not up or down the street, but across the yard next to it. Today even adults disappear when they get or give a stranger a ride. I watched a show about a serial killer that lured women from bars on the pretext of needing a ride.

Let's say you are out driving and decide to pull in somewhere public. Watch the area around you; if you see someone walking nearby and they change directions headed toward you, trouble is headed your way, exit real fast. This has saved me twice.

If some guy stands in front of you and says, "As far as I am concerned there is not a woman who does not enjoy being raped". Don't ask him to give you a ride home. I witnessed this and fortunately for her the police found them before he succeeded in raping her. Would not have happened without the phone call to the police I made.

I was walking up the street one day when a car with 5 guys in it stopped and asked a female walking behind me for directions. She had one foot in the car when I pulled her out.

If you are in public do not be fixated on your cell phone or another electronic device. Pay attention to your surroundings. Our brains are not set up to multi-task. Someone could easily approach you and grab you before you are even aware you are in danger. Pickpockets also target people who are not paying attention to their surroundings.

Always carry mace especially at night. There was a widely publicized abduction of a woman in Philadelphia that was recorded on video from a camera. She was abducted on a Sunday night and rescued Wednesday in Maryland. She had the fortitude to put up a struggle but things could have gone differently if she had mace to use.

Beware of men who say being raped is the same as having sex with someone. Rape is not the same as consensual sex, it is a crime of violence. I delivered newspapers as a teenager and one of my customers was a lawyer. I was collecting my money and there was a client crying streams of huge of tears. She asked me if I knew what it was like to be raped. I said, "No and I hope I never find out." I have seen a 30-year-old women cry about being raped when she was 12. Make no mistake about it rape and consensual sex are not the same. Never let anyone convince you otherwise if you have been raped. Some women at first do not realize this but you will eventually have to face your demons. Perhaps this is one reason why some women do not report rape.

Having been a Weapons Mechanic on the F-15 I learned about other things besides just the weapons system. Of importance to you is that the most vulnerable place that an attack may occur was from behind. There were two small mirrors attached to the canopy for the pilots to watch from. Always watch behind you also.

If anyone places a tray of cookies outside the men's room, don't eat any. Only two out of five men wash their hands before leaving.

As a rule, I never carry any amount of money large enough to hurt financially were it lost or were I mugged for it. It is not worth losing a life over – yours or the muggers – so it is best to just hand it over – don't try to be a hero.

If you are sitting at home and you notice that all your neighbors shut off all their lights at the same time, say like five minutes to 7:00 p.m. shut yours off too, really quick.

Tape recorders

Tape recorders are available everywhere. They come in many sizes, etc. They can be hidden in a room anywhere. Either by a stalker or you could leave on in your home to detect an intruder. Get a voice activated one for your use. Some are designed specifically so the motor cannot be heard and there's no click when the tape ends. Many are now small enough to be concealed on a person. Then there was the woman I had a few dates with that informed me on the phone that I had told her that I loved her. Then she tells me she is recording the conversation. In our state, you must inform someone if you are recording a conversation. I told her that you were supposed to do this before the fact and that I had never said I loved her and it could not be used against me. I wondered how a divorced mother of three boys could afford all the things she used to buy for them. I never dated her again. It is a sad day when you cannot tell a woman you love her without incriminating yourself.

Tape recorders along with other devices emit radio waves plus ultrasonic sound, which can be detected with the proper device. This device will vibrate when in the presence of a recording tape recorder, or even those digital recorders. The supplier I found had discontinued their model but they are out there. I can personally testify that the police have them in their stations. It would seem they might have something to hide because they do not like you using one on them. They will let you know, that they know. In some states, it is illegal to record a conversation without the other party knowing. In others, it is OK as long as one party knows. Others require that the other party be notified that you are recording them. If for business purposes, it is just plain proper for you to state this fact. To be safe, check your state's laws. However, I can't help but mention that if someone calls you and leaves a threatening or obscene message on your answering machine, they know it is being recorded.

I bought a voice recorder disguised as a flash drive called a "4GB USB Flash Drive Memory Stick Spy Digital Audio Voice Recorder". No, I am not a spy but a gadget geek. It even has a real working flash memory in it and can record while it is connected to a computer. The only clear difference from the real thing is that it has an on/off switch.

Trash

Yes, trash. One man's trash is another man's treasure. Actually, there is a wealth of information about you in your trash. Unobstructed routine access to your trash means you have no secrets. As of this writing, it is not a crime to pick up someone's trash off the curb. You give up any claim to it once you discard it on public land, and that includes trashcans. In 1988 the Supreme Court ruled (California vs Greenwood) that the 4th Amendment does not prohibit warrantless search and seizure of garbage which has been left for collection.

In short you no longer have an expectation of privacy or any ownership once you place your trash out for pick up. That does not just include the police. Stalkers and nosy neighbors can too. Leave your trash on your property and place it on the curb as late as possible to pick up time limiting the time it is legally available. Possibly it may become illegal to pick up someone else's trash. Even if that happens, that will not prevent someone interested in stealing your identity or stalking you, etc. Sexual assault is not legal either but it happens.

Speaking of trash, as I mention in the chapter about rape, do not leave anything with your address on it in a public trash receptacle. Rather you are a man or woman. It can only lead to grief. Keep track of your credit card receipts also.

Did you buy the shredder I recommended? They are very cheap compared to the cost of becoming an identity theft or rape victim. Shred, not tear up, those credit card offers you get in the mail. Unfortunately, there is software that makes the job of reassembling shredded documents so easy now. Being smart is not being paranoid. If it bothers you that much, move to some place where your paranoia will be justified.

Vehicles

Everyone recognizes the dual use vehicle as a portable home-made bomb. Not necessarily a problem unless you like to travel to Iraq. Well, terrorism has moved around the globe to the Boston Marathon so you may never be too safe anymore. Kidnappings are up in many foreign countries, so beware of this before traveling. Americans are a favorite target for someone wanting to make a statement or looking for quick cash. When in Rome, blend in with the Romans as much as you can. Try not to stick out as a tourist. Not going to work too well if you are in, say, China, hopefully you get the idea. Choose what country you travel too carefully. India for example has a poor reputation of protecting its own woman. A lot of high profile cases have come from India lately; I would be very caution of traveling there if I were a woman.

One young Indian woman was gang raped on a bus and later died. A Swedish tourist was gang raped and robbed while camping with her husband. Not to blame the victim but I have read of an American woman gang raped by 3 men she accepted a ride from while in India. I recently read a magazine article of a single woman's report of suffering PTSD from the constant sexual harassment from men while in India. As a good rule of thumb if a country does not value its own women what makes you think you as a tourist will be treated any better. When in a foreign country be especially cautious.

Most kidnappings or assassinations will occur while the victim is in transit in a vehicle. Your vehicle is a lethal weapon; learn how to use it. More importantly, do not be afraid to use it. I am not going to provide any instruction on this simply because it is not my area of expertise. Look for the appropriate material to learn how to use a car. Google "defensive driving" or visit Wikimedia.org which has some very good material on this.

There are plenty of publishing companies that deal with these different kinds of books, so look for one that specifically teaches you how to use a vehicle as a weapon.

The single most effective measure is to learn how to spot a potential problem. If you suspect you are being followed, drive in a figure eight and if the suspect vehicle takes the same path, then you are being followed. Laugh, but I have used this very effectively. OnStar would be very helpful in a situation like this. Second best is to always have a cell phone, but that's of little use if you do not know where you are. If you have enough money to own a car you have enough to own a cell phone. You can get a Trac phone for small change and buy yourself three months of air time and use it just for emergencies. Always know where you are. A GPS such as a Garmin can also give you the street name you are on. Always take your GPS with you, never leave it in your car. Try not to follow the same paths to or from a destination and vary your departure and or arrival times as well. This is especially helpful if you are a woman because you may be stalked without even knowing it until it is too late.

Always keep your vehicle in good repair so it will not leave you stranded or fail you at a most inopportune time. Keep tire pressures correct, as this will affect the vehicle's handling. Make routine inspections of your vehicle for tampering. Look specifically for electronic satellite trackers and other devices. A real bug detector would be best to locate one of these. I found one site that sold satellite trackers for $200. So they are not that expensive to obtain. With web access via cell phones it is now possible to track someone from anywhere. Did I mention that they are putting GPS in the cell phones now? One word of warning: these GPS trackers shut off when the vehicle is stopped, so you will need to drive it to determine if you have one attached. Or crawl under it to take a look, also look under your dash and seats. A mirror on the end of a stick will help. They are also available commercially.

Get one with an articulated end so you can move the mirror. The latest is a camera with a digital screen on a stick. Expensive to be sure especially compared to a mirror on the end of a stick

I found another one that was more of a data logger that had to be retrieved to recover the data. No monthly fee to monitor this one. They record speed position time/date and stops. Are also motion activated to conserve power. It was designed more for following cheating spouses and teenagers. Won't help you recover a stolen vehicle and quite likely is passive and does not radiate a signal to detect it with. You will have to physically search for this one. Very small so it can go in purses or backpacks as well. GPS jammers are also being made.

One more tip about tampering. Using common components readably available to the public a rapist can cause your car to stall wherever he wants. Sorry but this is so easy I am not going to tell you how just to convince you it is true. Familiarize yourself with the engine compartment so you will be better able to spot tampering or foreign devices. Do this every time after you have had someone unattended under you hood.

I was in a garage when a beautiful blond approached a mechanic and asked if this was possible. He said NO! But I intervened and provide a diagram of how it was done. She had been sent there from court and started to cry, when she read my written statement that she had been raped just like she said. Later he was found with 4 of these devices.

The Black Hat hackers conference lists pace makers and insulin pumps as being hack able. I have already mentioned baby monitors and garage doors but automobiles and even the human brain is next. With the advances in the technology in automobiles it is becoming a concern that your car can be hacked using that technology to disable or even cause a car to accelerate.

A bumper beeper can be attached to the underside of your vehicle with magnets. These devices can transmit a signal up to 5 miles making it extremely unlikely you could spot someone following you. Be diligent and regular about inspecting your transportation.

If not using electronics to detect them look for a device with an antenna. Special mirrors have been made to search the underside of a vehicle. Hardening a vehicle is expensive and only for rich or important people that have known reasons to be wary. Even the Pope needs the Pope mobile today. At the very least, I would recommend looking into reinforcing the front and rear bumpers for ramming.

Caltrops could also be used to stop a chase car. Do a search for Ninja supplies on the Internet. If the caltrops are not already black, paint them that color so they do not show up on the road and so be avoided. Unfortunately, they will also stop anyone else as well. If you are not using a remote release device just in front of the rear bumper, make sure that when you throw them from your vehicle they do not land under yours. Check to make sure it is legal to own them in your state.

Never hitch-hike or pick up hitch hikers. If you break down, cell phones make it too easy to call for help. The police will send a wrecker if you need one. I remember one of my grade school teachers telling me "If you have to hitch-hike make sure you (The guy) get in first". If not and the woman gets in first they could drive off with your woman leaving you. I remember giving a man and his wife a ride home. Total strangers and they lead me right to their home. I also remember that the wife got in first. When we got to their house I saw the husband get out and I heard the other door shut so I drove off. At the end of the drive way I had to back up to let a car on the street by. As I turned around the wife was still in my car.

I remember watching one of those reality cop shows you see on TV and a police officer had pulled over for a disabled car with a man and woman in it. The man kept looking into the wood so the officer went into the woods and found the body of the 70-year-old man who had picked them up hitch-hiking. Don't think you could not get raped if you were to pick up a hitchhiker.

In high school, I had a crush on a blonde in my chemistry class. One day driving to school I saw her and her sister walking to school so I pulled over to offer them a ride. They would not get in. When I saw them in class they said they were not allowed to hitchhike. One-day walking to school I saw them both hitchhiking and they got into a big gold car with one man driving.

I yelled out her name to make sure the driver knew they were seen with him. In class, her sister said he had driven right by the school and only stopped when she reminded him I had seen them.

Now let's look at the profit-making aspect of vehicles. The first thing that comes to my mind is the TV commercial where the guy tells you about the swoop and squat. Where a vehicle pulls ahead of you on the highway and another pulls in behind. That is the swoop part. Then the front vehicle does the squat part and simply stops, forcing you also to stop or hit him. Of course, the rear vehicle hits you. And you wonder why insurance is so high?

Coming home one night I noticed an accident on the other side of the highway. There was this little car underneath a big gold Cadillac. The Caddy's back bumper was just a foot shy of going through the windshield of the other car. Could not help but remember that TV commercial when the driver of the other car was smiling and waving to a car on my side of the highway. Here is a guy that could have lost his life but he has this big grin on his face.

In 1979, I owned a 76 Buick LeSabre. A married woman tried to seduce me with the intention of her husband catching us in the act. Their tenants informed me later that they wanted my car. You really don't have to have money to get sued. It is also wise to never have sex with another man's wife.

The first new car I bought was a 1984 Pontiac Sunbird. One day when out driving with the family, I spied an old guy standing next to the cross walk. Don't ask me why or what it was but I remember saying to myself, "I bet that guy is going to jump in front of me." So, I slowed down, given that this was an entrance ramp onto the highway. Sure enough, that guy started running out across the cross walk.

Fortunately, having slowed down enough, I managed to avoid running him over. Funny thing was, he had a limp. I said to him, "How much did you get for that limp?" Then I told him it would do him no good to jump in front of me because I did not have car insurance. When I got home, the police called me and wanted to know why I was driving without insurance. I told them what had happened and that what I had said / was to discourage the guy I'd encountered from pulling his insurance claim scam again. You see, I live in one of those mandatory auto insurance states. Then I told them to ask him how much did he get for the limp. Guess sometimes it is a good thing to be a little paranoid. Sometimes it is real after all.

In 1989, I owned a high-top conversion van. One day my then wife comes home and tells me she ran into a couple of guys. She also told me that when she tried to get someone to call the police using the CB radio in the van they took off. I told her to go report it to the police and that they were probably just a couple of jumpers. Well, a year and a half goes by and I get a call one day from a guy who claims to have been run into by my van. It all comes back to me and I asked him why he ran away and he said there was a warrant out for his arrest and he did not want to spend Christmas in jail.

Anyways, he claimed to have lost some teeth and his buddy suffered a broken leg. I also learned that if you do not report an incident like this to your insurance company within 30 days, the company does not have to pay out anything. At least the company investigated it and the two men's stories did not hold up.

Being tailed

Again, the single most important thing here is to be able to detect when you are being followed. I live in a state where you need police permission to even own a gun. One time when leaving the police station, I decided to do a side step. Leaning against the wall next to the door, it was fun to watch a police officer come out behind me and scan the parking lot looking for me. I wish I could have seen his face when I let him know I was behind him. If you try this with someone, you had better be able to handle the confrontation.

Vans are good vehicles to use for surveillance. So be suspicious of vans if you are suspicious of being followed. They are also the vehicles of choice of rapists.

One method available is to use a vehicle-tracking device (GPS). Another method available is to use an infrared LED that can be attached to the underside of a vehicle and observed with night vision devices. A company that markets these has been in business since 1980 and sells them for well over a hundred dollars. Meaning people are using them, just make sure it is not on you.

Then again, you may also want to include a search for one of these in your regular vehicle inspection. This is also a good way to follow your children on prom night. After all, you remember yours, right? So, if you want to make sure a certain car is not parked at a secluded location, this is a good way of being able to just happen by at the right time.

When Police Rape

A Tulsa County Deputy, an OHP trooper and an Oklahoma City police officer have all been charged with repeatedly raping and sexually assaulting women while on the job. One victim when asked why she did not immediately report the rape stated, "Who was I going to call the police?" She was just 17 but report every rape no matter who the perpetrator was; at once.

In response to the arrests of three law enforcement officials in Oklahoma for sexually assaulting women while on the job, an Oklahoma Highway Patrol trooper told women they can avoid getting raped by a cop if they simply follow traffic laws.

Capt. George Brown, a state trooper, shared a few tips for women in an interview with local NBC News affiliate KJRH. Brown told the KJRH anchor that women can keep their car doors locked and speak through a cracked window if a trooper approaches them. If the trooper asks a woman to get out of the car, Brown said, she can ask "in a polite way" why he wants her to do that.

But the "best tip that he can give," the anchor said on air of his interview with Brown, "is to follow the law in the first place so you don't get pulled over."

Brown said Oklahoma law enforcement officials are working to retain the public's trust. "There are entirely more good officers than there are the few bad apples that exist out there, and we want people to know that," Brown told KJRH. "We have a lot of good troopers, a lot of good officers out there doing a lot of good things daily, and we want to continue that and have the public continue their trust in us." As reported on Huffington Post.

There were posted replies to this article that pointed out if police officer wants to rape you they will just pull you over anyways. True but I believe the meaning was not to attract attention to yourself. Clothes do not make men rapists but I maintain that they are out there and your dress can attract their attention. Men are visual even though a victim's appearance is not a primary factor it never hurts of avoid standing out from the crowd. Never do I justify rape but less say you are the only woman walking down a busy street in a Bikini. If someone comes along looking for someone to rape who do you think they will grab first? It is like I have said else ware when traveling try to blend in with the crowd. Don't make yourself an easy target. Vulnerability and accessibility are the things most rapist look for in a potential vim. Victim's ages range from infant to elderly. Never wear skinny jeans.

I wish it were not true but police can and do rape and will continue to. What can be done? One idea I have is to make preliminary DNA testing a mandatory part of the application process to become an officer of the law. Then test all present officers to ensure they are not also rapists. It will also remove any sympathizers from the police forces that could aid a rapist to escape justice. They certainly do. I have express this idea to police officers before and it was not well received. If you are a police officer and feel this a bad idea you are probably a bad cop. You wear a uniform that you should be proud of and police your own to ensure that it is not tainted by the very thing you are sworn to prevent, crime.

Having been the air force, I wore a uniform that I was proud of too. Once I almost got into a fight with a marine because he thought my uniform was a joke being that I was in the Air Force. While I was in line at the on base Post office the man behind me was degrading all enlisted men and repeatedly said how he would not let his daughter date one.

Then he asked me if I would like to meet her. I said no I was so ashamed of the other enlisted men's behavior I just never felt I would be worthy in his eyes. Lastly there was one guy I told off big time because he was acting like a grade school kid. Even a 4-star general had disciplined him for it to no avail. Everyone wanted to know why I was so mad at him. I stated he had done that in public in front of me and he made me ashamed to wear this uniform. If you are a police officer and are reading this then respect your uniform and do not turn a blind eye to your fellow officer's crimes. Particularly rape. This is call the Blue Wall of Silence.

On Friday June 5 2015 a jury of 9 women and 3 men found Rajat Sharda guilty of rape while on duty as a Worcester Police officer the morning of August 6 2013.

A background check is done before a person can become a police officer. Being public servants every method available should be used to ensure the person receiving a badge is a moral and upright citizen that will not abuse it. Nor prey upon the people they swore to protect and serve. Presently not all methods available are being used to ensure just that. That will not change until DNA testing is utilized.

Shortly after I moved to Massachusetts in 1983 a Mass state trooper pulled two separate women over for speeding and raped them. I can still remember one victim on television stating how horrible it was. I could not understand then nor now whey he did not have his badge removed upon the first complaint. I was at my sportsman's club when a female senator was speaking and I told her about this incident and she stated, "There was nothing that could be done about it" this form a woman.

One more troubling thing is the lack of judges sentencing convicted rapists to prison. A flagrant example is District Judge G. Todd Baugh who imposed the 30-day sentence on Stacey Dean Rambold a teacher who raped then 14 year old Cherice Moralez, who committed suicide before her 17th birthday. I have seen and heard of this over and over but still cannot comprehend why. In my research, I came across an article about the 10 most corrupt states in the US. It stated that some were more corrupt than third world countries. One big problem was bribes. I am beginning to understand. Of course, if it is a police officer he might get a pass too. I don't care what they tell you one hand washes the other.

What can be done? In 39 states voters elect some or all of their judges. I support making all judges elected officials. It puts an accountability for their actions into the equation. I remember an incident in Virginia where a judge suspended a convicted rapist's 12-year sentence. Because it was an election year and this was made public on a local radio station he changed his mind and sent him to prison. I once talked to a chief justice here in the Worcester courts and challenged him to admit that he had also let rapists walk. He admitted that he had and that "Not thing one can happen to me". It is time that that was taken away from them. I wish a law could be made that if said rapist were to rape again when he should have been in prison the judge goes to jail for being an accessory.

The one thing I cannot say enough is to always report a rape or attempted rape. No matter who it is that perpetrated the attack. Go to an emergency room as soon as possible after the rape. You do not have to inform the police. Why would you if it was one of them? I strongly recommend reporting it to the FBI if it was a police officer. You can find their phone number in the front of any phone book.

Some rapist will make their cars look like police vehicles. Not so hard to do. If you are being pulled over by a vehicle that looks suspicious dill 911 on the cell phone I told you to always carry. Inform them you are being pulled over and are suspicious they will inform you if it is them. Did I mention to always know where you are? If it is not the real police that will be a good thing to know. Always keep your window down only a crack even if it is a real police officer. If you feel threatened or suspicious insist another officer is summoned. If they refuse or act threating pounding on your door get out of there. Worst case you get cited for trying to evade but even real police have raped women while on duty so it is better to be safe than sorry.

The following is copied from Wikipedia the free encyclopedia. I can't make this stuff up and could not put it better myself.

The **blue wall of silence,** also **blue code** and **blue shield,** are terms used in the United Stated to denote the idea of an unwritten rule that exists among police officers not to report on a colleague's errors, misconducts, or crimes. If questioned about an incident of misconduct involving another officer (e.g. during the course of an official inquiry), while following the code, the officer being questioned would claim ignorance of another officer's wrongdoing.

Police corruption is a form of police misconduct in which law enforcement officers break their social contract and abuse their power for personal or department gain.

The code is considered to be police corruption and misconduct. Any officers who engaged in discriminatory arrests, physical or verbal harassment, and selective enforcement of the law are considered to be corrupt. Many officers who follow the code may participate in some of these acts during their career for personal matters or in order to protect or support fellow officers.

All of these are considered illegal offenses and are grounds for suspension or immediate dismissal. Officers who follow the code are unable to report fellow officers who participate in corruption due to the unwritten laws of their "police family."

Police perjury "testilying" (in United States police slang) is when an officer gives false testimony in court. Officers who do not lie in court may sometimes be threatened and ostracized by fellow police officers. In 1992, the Commission to Investigate Allegations of Police Corruption (also known as the Mollen Commisioin) undertook a two-year investigation on perjury in law enforcement. They discovered that some officers falsified documents such as arrest reports, warrants and evidence for an illegal arrest or search. Some police officers also fabricated stories to a jury. The Commission found that the officers were not lying for greed but because they believed that they were imprisoning people who deserved it. Many prosecutors allowed police perjury to occur, as well.

Laws

Many police departments have their own code of conduct. The department trains new recruits and investigates police officers if they have a complaint from a civilian. There are also some state laws put in place to help protect civilians from corrupted officers. If the officer is found guilty, officers can be sued by the victim for damage caused by excessive force ("police brutality"), false arrest and imprisonment, malicious prosecution and wrong full death.

Federal laws strongly prohibit officer misconduct, including officers who follow the code by " testilying " or neglecting to report any officer who is participating in corruption. If an officer is in violation of any of the officer misconduct federal laws, only the federal government can issue a suit.

The police department is only responsible for preventing corruption among officers. If an officer is convicted, they may be forced to pay high fines or be imprisoned. To be convicted, the plaintiffs must prove that the officer was following the code or participating in negligence and unlawful conduct. It is often hard to convict an officer of following the code or other forms of corruption because officers are protected by defense of immunity, which is an exemption from penalties and burdens that the law generally places on other citizens.

"U.S. Supreme Court decisions have continually asserted the general rule that officers must be given the benefit of the doubt that they acted lawfully in carrying out their day-to-day duties, a position reasserted in Saucier v Katz , 533 U.S. 194, 121 S. Ct. 2151, 150 L. Ed. 2d 272 (2001)."

Cases

In 1970, New York City organized the Knapp Commission to hold hearings on the extent of corruption in the city's police department. Police officer Frank Serpico's startling testimony against fellow officers not only revealed systemic corruption but highlighted a longstanding obstacle to investigating these abuses: the fraternal understanding among police officers known variously as "the Code of Silence" and "the Blue Curtain" under which officers regard testimony against a fellow officer as betrayal.

In 1992, the Mollen Commission, commissioned to investigate reports of police corruption in New York City, noted that "The pervasiveness of the code of silence is itself alarming." One New York City police officer said, "If a cop decided to tell on me, his careers ruined... He's going to be labeled as a rat."

The following year saw the founding of the Civilian Complaint Review Board, an all-civilian board tasked with investigating civil complaints about alleged misconduct on the part of the New York City Police Department.

After that the International Association of Chiefs of Police made a code of police conduct publication and rigorously trained police officers. In 1991 Rodney King was brutally beaten by multiple police officers of Los Angeles Police Department. The officers involved were expected to have been following the "blue code". They claimed that the beating was lawful, but it was not until a videotape of the incident was released when it was confirmed that the officers had collectively fabricated their stories.

In the later 1990s, the FBI arrested 42 officers from five law enforcement agencies in 1998 on charges of conspiracy to distribute cocaine. In a 1998 report to U.S. Congressman Charles B. Rangel, the federal General Accounting Office (GAO) found evidence of growing police involvement in drug sales, theft of drugs and money from drug dealers, and perjured testimony about illegal searches.

History

The code and police corruption stems from the mid-to-late nineteenth century. The Pinkerton National Detective Agency were known for using police officers to violently end strikes. Many members of the Ku Klux Klan were police officers who protected each other when conducting racist acts. This later gave rise to the Civil Rights Act of 1964, which gave new protections to citizens who had long suffered discriminatory policing.

"Additionally, a string of landmark Supreme Court decisions during the era gave new force both to individual privacy rights as well as to curbs upon Police Power: highly influential cases resulted in the strengthening of Fourth Amendment rights against unreasonable Search and Seizure, evidentiary rules forbidding the use at trial of evidence tainted by unconstitutional police actions, and the establishment of the so-called Miranda Warning requiring officers to advise detained suspects of their constitutional rights. This criminalized officers who did not have the necessary paperwork to conduct a search or who were involved in falsifying documents or committing perjury.

Police culture

Police culture or "cop culture," as it is sometimes called by police officers, has resulted in a barrier against stopping corrupt officers. Police culture involves a set of values and rules that have evolved through the experiences of officers and which are affected by the environment in which they work. From the beginning of their career at their academies, police are brought into this "cop culture."

While learning jobs and duties, recruits will also learn the values needed to make it to a high rank in their organization. Some words used to describe these values are as follows: a sense of mission, action, cynicism, pessimism, machismo, suspicion, conservatism, isolation and solidarity. The unique demands that are placed on police officers, such as the threat of danger, as well as scrutiny by the public, generate a tightly woven environment conducive to the development of feelings of loyalty.

These values are claimed to lead to the code; isolation and solidarity leading to police officers sticking to their own kind, producing an us-against-them mentality.

The us-against-them mentality that can result leads to officers backing each other up and staying loyal to one another; in some situations, it leads to not "ratting" on fellow officers.

A *Los Angeles Times* report about the "Facebook manifesto" of Christopher Dorner, who was killed during a police manhunt after he went on a several day shooting spree in February 2013 in Southern California, observes: "When he arrived at the LAPD, he wrote, he found it a nest of racists. In the Police Academy, he complained about another recruit's use of a racial slur and was shunned.

On patrol with the LAPD, he complained that his training officer had kicked a mentally ill man, and in response the department conspired to destroy him. He had dared, he said, to violate the Code of Silence.

Whistleblowing

Whistleblowing (police officers reporting another officers' misconduct) is not common. The low number of officers coming forward may have to do with the understanding that things happen in the heat of the moment that some officers would rather keep personal. Another reason officers may hesitate to go against the blue code may be that challenging the blue code would mean challenging long-standing traditions and feelings of brotherhood within the institution. The fear of consequences may play a large role as well. These consequences can include being shunned, losing friends, and losing back-up, as well as receiving physical threats or having one's own misconduct exposed.

There are also forces that work against the code and promote whistleblowing. Many police officers do join the police force because they want to uphold the law; the blue code goes against this ideal. Some officers inform on fellow officers' misconduct, for less noble motives, such as to retaliate for mistreatment by fellow officers, to seek administrative recognition, or to prove loyalty to the department. Additionally, some officers are recruited by their administration to inform. If it is in an officer's job description to find misconduct by other officers, he or she is more likely to go against the blue code. Officers who go against the blue code may have a deal to avoid being fired or to receive immunity from prosecution. Some officers have also been known to break the code to sell a story to the media.

Levels of crime

Police officers are more likely to cover up certain kinds of errors by colleagues. One study showed that excessive use of force was the crime most commonly shielded by the code. Two studies suggest that some police feel that the code is applicable in cases of "illegal brutality or bending of the rules in order to protect colleagues from criminal proceedings," but not those of illegal actions with an "acquisitive motive."

Cases such as the Rampart scandal and many other police corruption cases demonstrate that blue code culture can extend to cover-ups of other levels of crime, acquisitive or not. The code has been called "America's Most Successful Stop Snitchin" Campaign," referring to cases where police covered up the misdeeds of fellow officers and where whistleblowers were harassed, professionally sanctioned, or forced into retirement.

Exposing the code

One method of preventing the code from penetrating the police force is exposure. Many states have taken measures in police academies to promote the exposure of the blue code. In most cities, before being admitted into the academy one must pass a criminal background check.

Through additional background checks, polygraph testing, and psychological evaluations, certain departments are better able to select individuals who are less likely to condone wrongdoing. In these departments, police are exposed to a basic training curriculum that instructs on ethical behavior; this instruction is reinforced in seminars and classes annually in some cases.

Several campaigns against the blue code or for making the blue code more visible in the public eye have taken place in the United States. One of the first of these campaigns was the Knapp Commission in New York (officially known as the *Commission to Investigate Alleged Police Corruption*) which was headed by Mayor John V. Lindsay in 1970. Over 20 years after the Knapp Commission the Mollen Commission was established in 1992 by New York City Mayor David Dinkins to investigate the nature and extent of corruption in the New York City Police Department NYPD, and to recommend changes to improve these procedures. These and other investigations have revealed details of the inner workings of the NYPD

Corrupt acts by police officers

Police officers have several opportunities to gain personally from their status and authority as law enforcement officers. The Knapp Commission, which investigated corruption in the New York City Police Department in the early 1970s, divided corrupt officers into two types: *meat-eaters*, who "aggressively misuse their police powers for personal gain", and *grass-eaters*, who "simply accept the payoffs that the happenstances of police work throw their way."

The sort of corrupt acts that have been committed by police officers have been classified as follows:

- **Corruption of authority**: When police officers receive free drinks, meals, and other gratuities, because they are police officers, whether intentionally or unintentionally, they convey an image of corruption.
- **Extortion/Bribery**: Demanding or receiving payment for criminal offenses, to overlook a crime or a possible future crime. Types of bribery are protection for illegal

activity, ticket fixing, alter testimony, destroying evidence, selling criminal information.

- The list goes on and on. Bribery is one of the most common acts of corruption.
- **Theft and Burglary** Is when an officer or department steals from an arrest and crime victims or corpses. Examples are taking drugs for personal use in a drug bust, and taking personal objects from a corpse at the scene of a crime. A theft can also within a department. An officer can steal property from the department's evidence room or property room for personal use.
- **Shakedowns**: Can be classified under theft and burglary. Stealing items for personal use from a crime scene or an arrest.
- **"Fixing"**: undermining criminal prosecutions by withholding evidence or failing to appear at judicial hearings, for bribery or as a personal favor.
- **Perjury**: Lying to protect other officers or oneself in a court of law or a department investigation.
- **Direct criminal activities** a law enforcement officer engages in criminal activity themselves.
- **Internal payoffs**: prerogatives and perquisites of law enforcement organizations, such as shifts and holidays, being bought and sold.
- **The "Frameup"**: the planting or adding to evidence, especially in drug cases.
- Ticket fixing: police officers cancelling traffic tickets as a favor to the friends and family of other police officers.

Prevalence of police corruption

Accurate information about the prevalence of police corruption is hard to come by, since the corrupt activities tend to happen in secret and police organizations have little incentive to publish information about corruption. Police officials and researchers alike have argued that in some countries, large-scale corruption involving the police not only exists but can even become institutionalized. One study of corruption in the Los Angeles Police Department (focusing particularly on the Rampart scandal) proposed that certain forms of police corruption may be the norm, rather than the exception, in American policing. In the UK, an internal investigation in 2002 into the largest police force, the Metropolitan Police, Operation Tiberius found that the force was so corrupt that "organized criminals were able to infiltrate Scotland Yard "at will" by bribing corrupt officers ... and that Britain's biggest force suffered 'endemic corruption' at the time".

Where corruption exists, the widespread existence of a Blue Code of Silence among the police can prevent the corruption from coming to light. Officers in these situations commonly fail to report corrupt behavior or provide false testimony to outside investigators to cover up criminal activity by their fellow officers The well-known case of Frank Serpico, a police officer who spoke out about pervasive corruption in the NYPD despite the open hostility of other members, illustrates how powerful the code of silence can be. In Australia in 1994, by 46 votes to 45, independent politician John Hatton forced the New South Wales state government to override the Independent Commission Against Corruption and the advice of senior police to establish a ground-breaking Royal Commission into Police Corruption However, in a number of countries, such as China, Pakistan, Malaysia, Russia, Ukraine, Brazil or Mexico, police corruption remains to be one of the largest social problems facing their countries.

"Noble cause corruption" and police

Noble cause corruption, as ethical corruption, is a departure from conventional discussions on police corruption, which typically focus on monetary corruption. According to the field of Police Ethics, noble cause corruption is police misconduct "committed in the name of good ends." In *Police Ethics* it argued that some of the best officers are often the most susceptible to noble cause corruption. According to professional policing literature, noble cause corruption includes "planting or fabricating evidence, lying or the fabrication and manipulation of facts on reports or through testimony in court, and generally abusing police authority to make a charge stick." According to Robert Reiner, a professor at the London School of Economics, stops based on statistical discrimination are also a form of noble cause corruption.

Effects of Police Corruption

Police corruption effects society, including political, economic, and sociological. The social aspect is perhaps easiest to define, because even one corrupt officer in a department can generate an overall distrust of the department (the Rotten Apple theory). This negative outlook on policing by citizens helps maintain an "us versus them" mentality among police, which only serves to further the rift between police and the public.

Police corruption, when brought to the public eye, increases pressures on departments by lawmakers to enact change from within. In 2013, the West Valley City, Utah police's narcotics unit was disbanded due to rampant corruption among its officers. These officers were found stealing small items from seized vehicles, taking evidence, and placing tracking devices on potential suspects' vehicles without warrants.

This action, like many others, not only increases distrust among the public, but lawmakers begin to feel pressure from the masses to remove officers and revamp entire departments.

Political Effects

Citizen involvement

Citizens within the jurisdiction look to lawmakers and justice officials to enact justice against the officers involved.

If the instance of corruption happens to fall on an election year, their re-election campaign may be lost. In areas such as Afghanistan, media exposure and citizen involvement in combating corruption is rarely seen. Rather, international officials step in to help eliminate corruption in the department.

Top-down discipline

Depending on the number of people involved and severity of the acts, the state executive or legislature may be compelled to demand that the department be scrutinized and its policies corrected. This can involve replacing individual officers, mid-level leadership, or asking for a resignation by the department chief. Disciplinary actions depend on the severity of the act, but typically result in disciplinary actions by the department and negative media coverage for the department. In 1970, the New York City Knapp Commission began holding officers and supervision accountable and institute real disciplinary actions for police corruption. In countries where corruption is a major issue, such as China and Russia, state government is often directly involved in investigating and disciplining cases of corruption.

Such as in the Chongqing gang trials, where police chief Wen Qiang was detained and put on trial for accepting bribes, rape, and other crimes during the Chongqing gang crackdown.

Social Effects

General distrust of police in the community

While political issues can easily be worked through, the social effect of police corruption is much harder to overcome. Citizens, especially those who or know someone who has been victimized by certain types of corruption, tend to see the police as more of an enemy. Similarly, police view citizens in the same light. Both issues have only been exacerbated by the War on Crime and War on Drugs. The "us versus them" mentality is especially prevalent among inner city minorities, where stereotyping and racial targeting seem to be the norm.

Rotten Apple Theory

This theory suggests that one bad cop ruins the entire department. A single officer can not only cause leadership to initiate investigations over entire sections or the department as a whole, but that one corrupt officer can bring a generally appreciated department to its knees in terms of public relations. People look at that one bad cop and assume, sometimes correctly (especially in this case, where several other officers were found to be committing similar violations) the entire department is corrupt and committing similar or worse acts.

Reduced effectiveness

Police corruption not only generates distrust among the populace, but undermines the criminal justice system as a whole. Judges and prosecutors may develop a negative opinion of officers who come to testify in cases, especially those who have a history of disciplinary action related to corrupt acts. The trustworthiness of officers who work in departments where corruption has been discovered is severely diminished, and even if the testimony they provide in court is an exact recollection of the events in question, a prosecutor or judge may choose to simply ignore these facts because of their association with a seemingly corrupt department. In the case of the Waldo, FL police, the entire department was disbanded partly due to allegations of corruption, meaning county law enforcement must take over where the city failed.

Economic Effects

Officer training

Should the corrupt act not be extremely severe, or the department decide discharge of the officer is unnecessary, those involved in corrupt acts may be charged to undergo remedial training. This could be inside or outside the department, and becomes another red mark on the already strapped budget of most departments. The cost of this remedial training pales in comparison to the cost of having to train new officers to replace those who are relieved of their duties, since these new hires will need to undergo initial academy training as well as whatever additional training the officer would require as they advanced in their career.

Investigations

Investigation and litigation costs may be high. These investigators are either part of their own department or taken from other squads (county sheriff investigating a city department, for example), or can be private entities. The department must also invest in retaining attorneys for both themselves and the officers involved.

One common form of police corruption is soliciting or accepting bribes in exchange for not reporting organized drug or prostitution rings or other illegal activities.

Another example is police officers flouting the police code of conduct in order to secure convictions of suspects—for example, through the use of falsified evidence. More rarely, police officers may deliberately and systematically participate in organized crime themselves.

In most major cities, there are internal affairs sections to investigate suspected police corruption or misconduct. Similar entities include the British Independent Police Complaints Commission. Police corruption is a significant widespread problem in many departments and agencies worldwide.

One problem I have with internal affairs departments is that they are made up of police officers. They do not always talk to anyone other than police officers when making investigations. Recourse, contact the FBI.

Technology available to the Police

Range R This device is a handheld radar that looks like a complicated stud finder. It can be used to detect movement inside a building as slight as breathing and will display how far away up to 50 feet. It will work through brick and reinforced concrete. It uses radio waves that work like a finely tuned motion detector. Others are more sophisticated and can display a 3d picture of the inside. One is capable of being mounted on a drone. These were developed for use in Iraq and Afghanistan for the military. The Supreme Court ruled that the Constitution bars police from scanning the outside of a house with a thermal camera unless they have a warrant. They specifically noted that the rule would apply to radar-based systems that were then being developed.

Stingrays, also known as "cell site simulators" or "IMSI catchers," are invasive cell phone surveillance devices that mimic cell phone towers and send out signals to trick cell phones in the area into transmitting their locations and identifying information. When used to track a suspect's cell phone, they also gather information about the phones of countless bystanders who happen to be nearby. Law enforcement agencies all over the country possess Stingrays, though their use is often shrouded in secrecy.

The ACLU as uncovered evidence that federal and local law enforcement agencies are actively trying to conceal their use from public scrutiny, and we are continuing to push for transparency and reform. (From ACLU web site).

I have also watched a video of how a network wireless box can be hacked to record the same data. Only with this the user data is still received. This is being shared so you the prey will be aware that this technology exists and will someday fall into the wrong hands.

The following is a quotation from the Yahoo Contributor network by Jennifer Weiss.

"The majority of rape cases go unreported for various reasons. The victim may feel it was her fault. She may fear the rapist would return or she may feel traumatized. No matter the reason a woman should always report a rape. Just the thought that you reported it and he could go to jail is more than enough. It gives a feeling of gaining control of your life and not letting the attack have power over you and your actions. I wish I had the courage to report my rape. It's one of my biggest regrets, don't let it be yours.

A lot of women don't talk about being raped because they feel dirty and as if the whole attack was her fault somehow. Try to remember that being raped is not your fault. Rape is a serious crime of violence and you didn't do anything to deserve it. The more you talk and express your feelings the easier it will be to handle the heartache. "Keeping secrets is not good.

I have always felt it best to confront your demons sooner rather than later." (My words) Again speaking out gives you control of your life and no longer gives him power over your thoughts and emotions.

The best thing anyone can do is to be knowledgeable and learn the basics to self-defense. You don't want to be defenseless when you are attacked in any way. If you are attacked, don't allow the attacker to gain control over you. Report it. Fight back in every way you can. A person can learn how truly serious this crime can be through real life experiences.

It's an issue that is overlooked and viewed as not as serious as other crimes like murder. As a society, we need to understand just how serious rape and other sexual assaults are.

Notes

Notes

Made in the USA
Columbia, SC
16 October 2017